BRAIN COMPATIBLE STRATEGIES

Second Edition

For information:

Corwin Press
A Sage Publications Company
2455 Teller Road
Thousand Oaks, California 91320
www.corwinpress.com

Sage Publications Ltd.
1 Oliver's Yard
55 City Road
London EC1Y 1SP
United Kingdom

Sage Publications India Pvt. Ltd.
B-42 Panchsheel Enclave
Post Box 4109
New Delhi 110 017 India

Printed in the United States of America.

ISBN: 1-890460-41-9

This book is printed on acid-free paper.

06   07   08   09   10   9   8   7   6   5   4   3   2   1

BRAIN COMPATIBLE STRATEGIES

Second Edition

Hundreds of easy-to-use, brain-compatible activities that boost attention, motivation, learning and achievement

ERIC JENSEN

CORWIN PRESS
A SAGE Publications Company
Thousand Oaks, California

Table of Contents

11/21/06

Using this Book

No single activity will turn a learner into an Albert Einstein, Quincy Jones or Martha Graham. Although any of the suggestions in this book will help the brain learn better, the activities do not stand alone. They are useful only within the broader context of a brain-compatible learning philosophy that:

- eliminates a sense of threat
- facilitates complex, real-life learning
- respects the uniqueness of each learner
- engages learners' emotions
- provides specific, immediate feedback
- understands the limits of the brain's attention span
- utilizes patterns during instruction
- promotes active, relevant, choice-driven learning
- applies meaning to abstract concepts

Not every suggestion is optimal for every age group. These brain-compatible strategies are purposely diverse; some are intended for professional trainers, some for teachers and some for adult learners. This wide variety of suggestions will further come in handy when you encounter the diversity of learners within a particular are group.

Using the book is easy. Browse through it and mark one or two ideas you'd like to try and put them into practice. If an activity seems like a poor fit for your students, relax. With a simple twist, the suggestion may still work for your particular audience. Adapt any idea to suit your personality and presentation style.

Your learners will become more motivated, understand things better, enjoy the learning process, recall more material and apply what they've learned to events the real world. Even the gradual introduction of one or two strategies a week will have an enormous impact on learners after just a year's time.

As you experiment, make a few notes about your reaction to the strategy, when you plan to use the idea again or what you might want to change the next time. You have permission to write in this book—that's part of the learning process. Your personal commentary will make this a much more valuable resource. Enjoy marking it up!

Activity List

Activity List continued...

Preface

Brain-Compatible Strategies, Second Edition, is still packed with fun suggestions and strategies to turn your classroom into a brain-friendly place. *Brain-Compatible Strategies* is still a great introduction to the field of brain-based learning. And *Brain-Compatible Strategies* is still the handy guide you can flip through for activities and ideas to implement right away? So what's different? The book is better than ever!

A team of principals and school administrators reviewed the first edition of this book and made recommendations for improvement. The book is easier to read, the explanations easier to understand and the suggested activities easier to implement. Also, the activities have been categorized to help you quickly narrow down your choices so you can pick the right strategy at the right time. These added details and clarified instructions make this handbook a very valuable, very user-friendly teaching tool.

Put your learners on the fast track to better learning with practical instructional strategies based on sound principles of neuroscience. The ideas and suggestions in this book work because they are based on the way our brains actually function and the way people actually learn. If you want to learn more about why these activities work and where to find out more about brain-based learning, the resources listed at the back provide a broader foundation to this important education field.

Now, go stimulate neural growth—and have fun doing it!

Activate the Young-at-Heart Brain

Surprisingly, many common games are good for the brain, but solving problems is the number one, all-time best activity for brain growth (increasing neural connectivity, the number of glial cells and overall brain mass). The best problems to solve meet the following conditions: 1) They are novel (you must change the content and process of solving problems often); 2) they are challenging (make sure the difficulty level is appropriate for your audience); 3) they are non-threatening (everyone should want to contribute); and 4) they stimulate emotions (learners should feel anxiety, joy, anticipation, surprise or celebration). Play children's games as-is with children; customize their rules or content to play with adolescents or adults.

Suggestions

✔ **Choosing a game:** Look to board games for ideas. (There are hundreds!) *Monopoly*, *Clue*, *Trivial Pursuit*, *Chutes and Ladders* and chess are all popular and easily adapted. Also consider other kinds of games, like Around the World, *Jeopardy*, Twenty Questions, crossword puzzles, tic-tac-toe, Bingo, dominoes or even a game of hangman with spelling words.

✔ **Playing a game:** Simply playing a game with traditional rules can excite the brains of young learners. The challenge and opportunity to solve problems is the best exercise for enriching their gray matter. But add variety—have the students work in pairs to devise a game strategy, design minor variations or revise the rules. Turn students who win the most into game consultants and circulate them around the room to teach their classmates how to win.

✔ **One example of an adapted game:** Use *Monopoly* as a review with adolescents or adult learners. Put the class in teams of four and give them one hour to substitute, alter and re-label the game to match the content of the course. The first time you try this with your class it might not go very smoothly. Remember that it's the process that's important, not the slick polish of a final product. Once teams have finished their version of the game, have them swap game boards and play each other's versions.

Greater Meaning from Multiple Contexts

As the brain learns, it stimulates cells to grow branch-like extensions called dendrites. Each dendrite is another neural pathway by which cells can connect to each other. What we commonly call a "greater depth of meaning" really refers to cells making more connections and finding new pathways to other cells. Maximize the number of connections they make by providing multiple contexts for learning the same thing. The more ways we learn something—in a variety of contexts, using multiple intelligences, triggering emotions through several types of media—the better. This breadth of experience will allow us to more easily access what we learned in the future.

Suggestions

✔ Teach a topic in several different ways. Encourage peer teaching, the use of computers, graphic organizers and personal investigation.
✔ Facilitate more group work. Make sure students interact in groups at least one a day.
✔ Invite guest speakers, take field trips and plan classroom events. These novelties contribute to greater diversity of learning.
✔ Switch classes with another teacher. Not classrooms—classes! You'll all enjoy the change of personality, routine and content.
✔ Share personal information (yours and the students') during discussions or group work. Have students perform a variation of what you usually do in class or at home (make sure it's something fun!).

Which ideas did I try today? What were the results?
What will I *do differently* next time?

_____

_____

_____

Specific Feedback Accelerates Learning

Enhance learning by dramatically increasing the quantity and quality of feed-back—increasing feedback is the best way to increase the number of dendrites in the brain. The brain is a complex organ that thrives on information; corrections allow it to improve its learning and survival behaviors. (Sadly, some college and university professors use just a mid-term and final exam for evaluating student progress.) Make it your personal and professional promise to provide some kind of feedback to students every thirty minutes. This will, of course, be impossible to do if you are the only person giving feedback; if you have thirty-five students in your classroom, you just don't have the time. Fortunately, feedback can origi-nate from many other sources.

Suggestions

✔ Provide ways that students can find answers to their work through self-correction. For instance, grade some tests and quizzes on the spot. Or, use tools that provide immediate feedback during a practicing activity, like Holey flash cards for mathematics facts.

✔ Have student use checklists and timelines to set daily or weekly goals. Then, have them check their own progress.

✔ Assign to students the task of summarizing the previous day's class content in one page or less. Then, have them write three quiz questions and test a neighbor's knowledge.

✔ Help students create a performance or grading rubric. Allow students to assess themselves against this rubric so they know exactly how they are doing.

✔ Use a variety of tools to provide feedback to students, including audio and video recordings, a mirror, partner work or fishbowl activities. Discuss with students what they learned about their performance from each type of feedback.

✔ Establish rituals to deliver feedback. They will give students the opportunity to interact and receive evaluation from a peer. For example, have student pairs assess each other after each assignment and conclude with a high five or sincere verbal thanks.

All Work and No Play…

Childhood games are an excellent way to review content material. Some games are suited to repetition and drill (instead of boring worksheets); others are perfect for raising the level of feel-good amines in the brain, like dopamine and norepinephrine. In the right amounts, these biological "uppers" improve working memory and cognition. Musical Chairs is one of those childhood games that seems silly in the classroom but, with a few twists, transforms it into a brain-friendly place.

Suggestions

Have participants bring their chairs into a circle (one will be removed at the start of the game). To start the game, ask everyone to stand up and perform some easy, interactive task, like introducing themselves to a new classmate, giving positive affirmations, reciting one fact from the day's lesson, finding people who were born in the same month or simply shaking hands with everyone. Play bright, cheerful music in the background.

Stop the music after ten to twenty seconds have passed. As in the traditional rules of Musical Chairs, participants run for an empty chair to sit in. But the last person standing doesn't lose the round—she becomes the new music master. You will join the game and she will start and stop the music (like you did), once she has demonstrated she is worthy of the responsibility by successfully completing some task.

Make sure all the participants are able to do the task (see the ideas below) and make sure it is not embarrassing. It is critical for this activity to be totally non-threatening. Give participants time for reflection and preparation before you start, no matter what version of Musical Chairs game you are playing:

✔ **Getting to know you:** Participants introduce three other people to the rest of the group.
✔ **Review:** Participants state one or two things they learned in the previous lesson.
✔ **Self-disclosure:** Participants share with the group something about themselves that others probably do not know.
✔ **Storytelling:** Participants add installments to a story that was started previously.
✔ **Concept connecting:** Participants connect one new idea to another.

Learning with Feeling

Research tells us that cognition and emotions, although they originate in different parts of the brain, are so intertwined that they influence each other. Their separate paths of influence intersect in the orbitofrontal cortex (the lower area of the frontal lobes).

Pay close attention to students' feelings before starting a lesson. Emotional states trigger either activity or inactivity; are students in the right frame of mind for what you want? Making emotional connections to material is the primary way of making meaning out of it—emotional investment drives attention and motivation, too. Finally, learning is much more memorable if it is attached to strong feelings. If students have a good feeling about what they've learned, they'll recall it later and will want to come back for more.

Suggestions

✔ Put learners into a positive state before learning. Activate their curiosity, trigger past feelings of success or create anticipation for the fun they are about to have.

✔ Actively engage student emotions while learning. Use drama, storytelling, music or movement. Read a story while a movie soundtrack, classical music (like Haydn) or romantic music (like Tchaikovsky) plays in the background. Or, ask students to dramatize what they've learned by scripting and performing a commercial for the material.

✔ Use intense intellectual or physical activities like debates, student presentations, humor or tug-of-war. Allow students to pick their debating partner and decide which side of an argument they want to speak on. Give them each sixty seconds to argue their point of view as best they can. Then, have them switch points of view.

✔ Role model expressing emotions with poignant personal examples. The more you show that emotions can be strong (but appropriate), the safer you make it for students to express them.

✔ Celebrate after completing a learning segment with some cooperative group ritual that acknowledges or congratulates another team. Incorporate music, chanting, clapping rhythms or silly awards (like for "The Person Who Sharpened His Pencil the Most").

Escape from the Sacred "Learning Box"

The brain craves stimulation, change and novelty. Unfortunately, many teachers and trainers crave control and predictability. As a result, you have classes and seminars that stay in the same "learning box" (the classroom or training room) day after day. Too much predictability, however, can inspire discipline problems (from learners trying to break the monotony). Even students exercising self-control may get bored; all of them experience a drop in heart rate, alertness levels and blood circulation.

It is easy to wake up the brain with fresh air (even just for two minutes). Bring your class to unusual locations and invigorate their thinking and learning. Physical movement and changes in the routine both stimulate interest and move freshly oxygenated blood to the brain. New stimulation, a novel location and fresh ideas may be just what you need to bring your subject to life.

Suggestions

✔ Ask participants to select partners. Assign a "pair-share" activity to complete as the partners take a five-minute walk outside the building (if the weather permits) or through empty hallways inside the building.

✔ Take students outside of the classroom to study something from a different point of view. Trigger ideas related to objects you see as you walk. For example, use shapes of the building to talk about mathematics, the style of the architecture to talk about history or culture or the process of construction to philosophize about the nature of motivation and human vision. Have students bring paper for jotting down questions and notes to discuss when you return to class.

✔ Role reversal stimulates energy and interest without learning the room. Assign small parts of the day's content to groups or teams for the purpose of teaching it to the entire group. Provide them a template for their presentations, tools, plenty of support and a deadline. After the presentation, allow other students to offer feedback.

Which ideas did I try today? What were the results?
What will I do differently next time?

_____

_____

_____

Remove Barriers to Learning

What we call "barriers to learning" may be any of several things within the brain. Students may have a learning condition such as (but not limited to) dyslexia, learning delays, acalculia, attention deficit, fetal alcohol or learned help-lessness. More commonly, however, is the presence of contradictory, competing or erroneous prior knowledge that is both complex and persistent. Prior knowl-edge exists as neural networks in the brain. Because the networks may consist of thousands of neurons, they're difficult to restructure. Rebuild incorrect prior knowledge with targeted, specific knowledge over a long duration of time.

Emotions can set up barriers, too. If we have memories of a strongly negative emotional content, they may activate inhibitory neurotransmitters instead of excitatory neurotransmitters and discourage connections (and therefore new learning). We've all heard of people complaining about their math hang-ups or foreign language problems—their brains block those types of learning. The secret to removing these barriers is to recognize them and approach learning through alternative, more open channels.

Suggestions

✔ Make a list of the barriers your learners might have in the areas that you teach, like content blocks (math- or language-phobia) or process blocks (reluc-tance to try because of a belief in ultimate failure).

✔ Hold discussions with learners about what they already know. Ask them to explain how they know it to be true. Prompt as much detail as you can.

✔ Have students create graphic organizers of everything they already know about a subject. (If they draw them on transparencies, you can easily show them to the whole class.) Use student prior knowledge (and misinformation) as a springboard for discussion about the upcoming topic.

✔ Present new information in a hierarchical format (outlines or trees) to empha-size relationships and maximize accuracy of main ideas and details.

✔ Create and post colorful peripheral posters that can positively influence learners: *Math is E-Z and Fun!* or *I Can Learn Anything*.

✔ Make learning a by-product of another activity. Learn math by playing Bingo or planning the redecoration of an apartment. Learn languages by taking learners to a restaurant or traveling abroad.

Active Learning

There are many reasons to engage learners physically. First, it strengthens far more neurons than does a sedentary experience like a lecture. Second, it gives you and the learners plenty of feedback on what they know and don't know. Third, physical movement is usually motivating and rewarding. Most students are a bit of a ham and are happy to learn in alternate ways. Finally, kinesthetic involvement engages emotions, builds problem-solving skills and aids learning by encapsulating information in the brain so it can be recalled more easily later.

Suggestions

- ✔ **Add-ons.** Invite one person to come up to the front of the room and act out or pose as some idea or concept that they have learned from the lesson. One by one, have other students come up and join the impromptu living sculpture until they form one giant human representation of what they've been learning.
- ✔ **Body machines.** Small teams re-enact the functioning of a common machine (like a car, ATM, bar code scanner or dishwasher).
- ✔ **Body talk.** Ask a volunteer to come to the front of the room and demonstrate some physical trick they can do (keep it clean!). Some people are very double-jointed; others can roll their tongues, wiggle their ears or even turn hand springs or tap-dance. This activity is an excellent ice-breaker.
- ✔ **Commercial breaks.** Each student team (or pair) is assigned or chooses a review topic. After ten minutes of prep time and rehearsal, they act out a commercial for the material that they've been learning. Give them thirty seconds to be funny, bizarre, cute, sappy or exciting—whatever it takes to "sell" the "product" of knowledge and get everyone else to remember it.

Which ideas did I try today? What were the results? What will I do differently next time?

_____

_____

_____

Learn by De-Briefing Failures

Learning comes in many forms. We learn implicit knowledge (basic things we just seem to know) from doing an activity and describing what we learn. Research suggests that human subjects learn declarative knowledge (explicit knowledge that can be shared with another person) from unsuccessful performances. In other words, doing it right the first time produces no new learning but failure encourages us to learn better the next time. Research subjects who described themselves as clueless about a process experienced a breakthrough of comprehension only four to six attempts later.

Implicit and declarative knowledge can develop at the same time. Failure can be a great learning strategy if it is accompanied with fine-tuning during the process of repeated attempts (with specific feedback) instead of just talking and hearing about it.

Suggestions

✔ During motor learning, ask participants to verbalize what they are doing while they are actually doing it. Have them work with a partner to increase accountability.

✔ Keep the feedback coming but provide sufficient time for students to learn from mistakes. Often, a breakthrough is just around the corner. Remind students that it is acceptable to fail repeatedly as long as they keep trying.

✔ Help your students understand the difference between implicit knowledge (your body knows how to do something) and declarative knowledge (you know how to explain it). Set a goal for students to learn both ways of understanding the concepts and ideas of the class.

Which ideas did I try today? What were the results? What will I do differently next time?

_____

_____

_____

Integrated, Contextual Curriculum

There are many ways to learn. Learning in a real-world context, like going to a county fair, renting an apartment, publishing a magazine, visiting a retirement community or riding a bike, provides far more information to the brain than knowledge offered out of context, or information that has been broken up into disparate pieces and presented one at a time. Imagine learning to ride a bicycle by taking classes in mechanics, road safety, neighborhood geography, social structure, first aid and courage. We'd never even want to try it and we certainly wouldn't enjoy the process. Most of us just jumped on a bicycle and figured it out. Smells, spatial landscape, sounds and dozens of other sensory details that make up a total experience contribute to further layers of understanding and make new knowledge easier to recall. In the classroom, make learning as experiential and hands-on as possible.

Suggestions

✔ Pick a single theme to use for several months, one that breaks easily into many multidisciplinary sub-topics like "Change," "Shapes," "Growing" or "Perspectives." If possible, work with teachers of other subjects to develop content into a full-fledged thematic unit across the curriculum.

✔ Run a lemonade stand one week during lunch breaks or tackle something as complex as a real estate finance, purchase and renovation to teach mathematical skills. To teach literature, select a work with universal resonance that triggers many other paths of learning; Melville's *Moby Dick*, for example, encompasses global travel, economics, mythology, cross-cultural friendships and ship-building. During geography class, have students plan an around-the-world trip. Create foreign-language comic books, tourist guides or learn how to become interpreters for immigrants.

✔ Give learners the choice to pursue several directions within a unit. That way, they can always pick something personally interesting or relevant.

✔ Incorporate multidisciplinary tangents whenever possible—it always happens in real life. If your class is studying a river, also teach its geological history, local geography, ecology and the cultures of the people that live nearby.

✔ Open up your classroom to guest speakers, on-location visits, computers, group interaction and popular media.

Ball Toss Boosts Thinking

A brain-compatible ball toss game encourages problem solving, cooperation, self-discovery and physical movement. It also provides you and your students the chance to think and act quickly in a safe environment. Set a learning objective for students to complete as they toss the ball to each other, asking and answering questions. Play lighthearted, fast-tempo instrumental music in the background as they toss the ball.

This game works best with teams of five or six students facing each other in a circle six to eight feet across. Toss something harmless, like a balled-up pair of socks, a Koosh ball, a small stuffed animal or a tightly wadded sheet of newspaper. The rules of play are easy to remember: 1) Always throw the ball underhanded so it stays within the circle but arcs above the head of the person who is catching it. 2) Take your time responding to questions but only speak when you are in possession of the ball. 3) Avoid the same consecutive answers. 4) Do not toss the ball to the person next to you or to the person who tossed you the ball.

After about two minutes of game play, tell each group to change their objective (perhaps to ask each other questions about something they learned the week before). Two minutes later, change their objective again. Play no longer than six minutes.

Suggestions

✔ **With children:** With every toss of the ball, students start or continue a story, spell words one letter at a time, recite math facts, list state capitals or former presidents or any items they are currently studying.

✔ **With adolescents or adults:** With every toss of the ball, students present opposing ideas on a topic, invent test questions, introduce themselves to each other, review content or training objectives or add on to a brainstorming list.

Which ideas did I try today? What were the results? What will I do differently next time?

_____

_____

_____

Let Learners Create Their Own Meaning

The brain thrives on meaningful information, not random information. What makes things meaningful to your brain? 1) Assembling disconnected pieces of information into a larger pattern to highlight relationships and connections. 2) Stimulating either positive or negative emotions. 3) Impacting a learner's personal life. Without meaning, learners lose interest and intrinsic motivation to succeed wanes. Although you, as a presenter, have no real power to make a concept meaningful to another person, you can encourage the development of meaning.

Suggestions

✔ Provide time to discuss in pairs or small groups the relevance of new information. Graphic organizers are excellent ways to record thoughts and feelings; creating mnemonic devices helps learners remember lots of new information at once.

✔ Purposely engage student emotions during the process of learning by making material sad, suspenseful or dramatic. Use celebrations, debates, music, role-playing or theatrics to evoke emotions.

✔ Connect learning to closely held desires of the learners: security (younger learners and older adults), peer acceptance and identity (adolescents), autonomy (young adults) or respect and achievement (adults). Use discussion, journaling or other methods to bring these values into every lesson.

✔ Ask learners to find three ways new information relates to their own lives. They might describe a trip they've taken, name a television show they've recently watched or relate an autobiographical incident.

✔ Schedule time to reflect and write in journals about the topic. Encourage your students to be personal and go into detail about their feelings or connection to the issues.

Which ideas did I try today? What were the results? What will I do differently next time?

_____

_____

_____

Cross Laterals "Unstick" Learning

The right side of the brain controls the left side of the body and vice versa. To look at it another way, if you activate the right side of the body, you activate the left side of the brain (and vice versa). When learners get stuck, it is usually for one of two reasons. When the left brain is stuck, the learner is an analytical quagmire. He says, "I tried everything! I did this, I did that and I just can't seem to find my way out of this problem." When the right brain is stuck, the learner is overwhelmed; when you inquire what she is stuck on, she answers, "Everything! I'm hopelessly lost!"

Fortunately, there is help for both learners. Our brains are better problem-solvers when they use both hemispheres. Hormonal fluctuations trigger stronger blood flows to different sides of the brain during the day. This alternation of left-to-right-to-left brain dominance is normal, but you'll want to encourage students to use of both sides of their brain for their best learning. Cross-lateral activities force the brain to talk to itself from both hemispheres. Because the right side of the brain controls the left side of the body and the left side of the brain controls the right side of the body, movements that cross the body activate both hemispheres at once.

Suggestions

✔ Alternate touching each hand to the raised opposite knee (or hip or elbow or heel) about ten times.

✔ Give yourself a pat on the back on the side opposite to the hand you are using. Then, switch.

✔ Touch your nose with your right hand and hold your right ear with your left hand. Switch hands and ears three times as fast as you can.

✔ Try "Lazy Eights" from *Brain Gym®* by Paul Dennison and Gail Dennison (1994: Edu-Kinesthetics). With your hand curled into a "thumbs up" sign, trace horizontal figure eights at eye level. Extend your arm completely and make the loops as large as possible, crossing in front of your nose. Follow your thumb with your eyes (without moving your head). After three figure eights, switch arms. Then, trace figure eights with both hands at once (keep your thumbs together as they follow the same pattern).

More Questions Than Answers

The brain is more receptive to questions about new knowledge than it is to answers. Why? Curiosity is a distinct physiological state that triggers changes in our posture and eye movements and promotes chemical reactions that are advantageous to learning and recall. When we ask ourselves questions, the brain continues to process them even after they're answered. To your brain, the process is far more important than the outcome.

In short, you increase your capability of learning when you ask questions and your brain will continue to ponder the questions even after answers are found. This may explain why a laboratory or theoretical scientist remains dedicated to the pursuit of one idea for years. The quest for knowledge, not the knowledge itself, is what is so exciting.

Suggestions

✔ Have students generate questions before you introduce a topic. Post them around the room, publish and distribute them or record them for review at the conclusion of the unit. KWL charts (what the learner already *knows*, what the learner *wants* to know and, later, what the learner has *learned*) are particularly suited to this purpose.

✔ Write anticipatory questions about an upcoming lesson and put them in a hat or basket. Each day, pick one question and solicit answers from the group.

✔ Create a "question of the day" board and update it regularly with contributions from you or the students.

✔ Ask students to write the questions for the next test (and use some).

✔ Encourage questions and provide clear, thoughtful answers. Turn questions into interesting, divergent paths of exploration.

✔ Turn content into question for games based on popular quiz shows (like *Jeopardy*) and play them.

Which ideas did I try today? What were the results? What will I do differently next time?

_____

_____

_____

Challenge the Brain

Energy levels ebb and flow in the brain throughout the day, partly because of varying glucose levels. The brain uses glucose as fuel; mentally taxing work depletes glucose in the areas that are activated. Also, when the body is in a resting state (like sitting still and listening), blood circulation and heart rate drops. Physical movement and mental stimulation are the best ways to spur the brain into action. They raise amine levels and can improve memory and attention. Every educator should have on hand dozens of activities to wake up students whenever they look tired or sluggish. Here are two suggestions to get you started.

Suggestions

- ✔ **Touch Gold!** In sequence, students find and touch 5 things that are gold, 4 things that are silver, 3 things made of glass, 2 things made of leather and 1 shoe on someone else's foot. Everything they touch must be at least ten feet apart. Or, add variations according to content. For math, have students touch objects with the characteristics of right angles, cylinders, cubes or rectangles, or according to length and height. They can touch objects according to their texture, color, weight or rarity in a science class. As part of a history lesson, ask them to touch things that could have been found during a certain era. For English, have them touch objects that must be capitalized if spelled out. In economics, they might touch items in order of value or cost.
- ✔ **Circle run-ons:** Students form groups and stand in a circle. Give each team a topic for review and designate a leader to start a sentence about the topic without finishing it. The person on the leader's left continues the sentence but leaves it hanging for the next person. The goal of this activity is to keep the sentence going around the circle as long as they can. The person who ends the sentence gets a good-natured groan from teammates, but also gets to start the next sentence. To add variety, have the groups walk in a circle as they talk or have students stand on one leg until it is their turn to speak.

Which ideas did I try today? What were the results? What will I do differently next time?

_____

_____

_____

Engage Spatial-Episodic Memory

Your brain has two parallel visual systems that record everything you see as either content (what you see) or context (where you see it). Your brain sorts this incoming data by whether it is embedded in content or embedded in context. If you read a paragraph about planting flowers in a gardening book, you learn only content. If you go to your garden and follow the directions on the back of a seed package to plant flowers, you learn from context. You can learn through both channels but the second, contextual way is far more memorable.

All learning is contextually embedded in some way. The more similar contexts for learning are to each other, however, the harder it will be for the brain to retrieve information—imagine naming all your computer files the same thing! Distinct locations and circumstances provide the brain many more identifying clues for efficient retrieval later. The more you utilize this characteristic of spatial-episodic memory, the greater recall your learners will have. Context provides dozens of sensory cues that can better trigger memory.

Suggestions

✔ **Change the location of learning**: Rearrange desks so students face another side of the room. Or, change how and where students are seated when they learn—put them on the floor one day, maybe stand them up on another. If you have the luxury or opportunity, teach outdoors during a sunny afternoon or take field trips.

✔ **Guest speakers**: Even a guest speaker from your own school can add variety to your class.

✔ **Props, costumes and special music**: The best props and costumes are the ones the students use, not what you use. Keep a big box of props in the back of your room.

✔ **Special events**: Plan curricular themes or other events to associate learning with special days. Take advantage of holidays, changes of season, different colors or milestone celebrations.

Active Learning II

Monitor the alertness or fatigue levels of your learners. If they have just finished a learning consolidation activity or if their energy flags, switch activities to wake them up and catch their attention. The following four activities can raise energy, activate focus and add some extra fun to the day!

Activity breaks are best used once every two or three hours for students from grades two through five. Younger students need more, older students fewer. No matter what age, spend no more than ten minutes on the activity before returning to learning.

Suggestions

✔ **Clapping games:** You start a clap or rhythm and students pass it around the room until everyone is clapping the same rhythm. Then, the first student starts a different clapping rhythm and others follow suit. Clap a pattern, listen and repeat the pattern. This also trains memory and music skills.

✔ **Gordian Knot:** Teams of six to eight people stand facing each other in a tight circle. Everyone reaches into the circle and clasps the hands of two other people. Their task is to untangle the knot they have made without letting go of anyone's hands.

✔ **Lap sit:** Everyone in the group stands shoulder to shoulder in a close circle, then turns so they are looking at the back of the person that was to their right. At the instructor's cue, everyone holds the shoulders of the person in front of them and slowly sits down on the lap of the person behind them. This game works for groups of any size—even really big ones.

✔ **Pass a face:** Everyone stands in a large circle. One person makes a crazy face to the person on his or her left, who in turn passes it to the left until it has traveled all the way around the circle. Then, another person passes another face. To vary the game, pass one face to the left and another to the right (they will meet halfway around!) or pass a gesture or sound.

Which ideas did I try today? What were the results? What will I do differently next time?

_____

_____

_____

Visuals and Peripherals Impact Learning

The human brain can register more than 36,000 images per hour; your eyes can absorb thirty million bits of information per second. It makes sense to take advantage of these amazing organs hungry for pictures and moving images when you are delivering instruction, especially in light of the fact that most of the brain's learning is non-conscious. In fact, studies of the impact of peripherals (posters, pictures, drawings and symbols displayed on walls around the room) suggest they are powerful influences on the brain. The effects of direct instruction diminish after about two weeks but the effects of your visuals and peripherals continue to increase during the same time period.

Suggestions

✔ Display colorful, inspirational, symbolic posters (with topics about reaching the peak or a mountain, the value of teamwork, the thrill of discovery or the accomplishments of historical figures). Ask students to bring them in or make them, or periodically swap posters with other teachers.

✔ Graphically organize the content of an upcoming lesson into a poster. Have students copy it in ways that are personally meaningful.

✔ Post work from student groups, rather than individuals, on the walls.

✔ Hang positive affirmations ("Your success is assured.") for learners to read. Ask them to create their own positive messages.

✔ Encourage students to design murals, mindscapes or "positive" graffiti for the walls of the room. These posters can be used for a variety of purposes, like content review or how to build relationships with other people.

✔ Use overhead transparencies, flip charts or other visuals while lecturing. Enlist two students, one on each side of you, to map what you are saying while you are saying it. Create a continuous, graphically organized record of class presentations. Rotate volunteers so everyone gets the chance to participate.

✔ Accompany learning with short video clips (from three to seven minutes in length) with powerful visual images to enhance retention and understanding. After showing part of a video, discuss the images and content with students and tie it directly to new and prior information.

The Real Power of Music

Brain research conducted at the University of California at Irvine tells us two important things about the brain. First, music can charge and energize our brain. When music harmonizes with our own rhythms, we are energized by it. Some research suggests our brain gains even more energy from certain frequencies (about 8,000 Hz). Second, music has been found to boost intelligence. Certain Mozart compositions have helped learners raise their intelligence scores on spatial-temporal reasoning after just ten minutes of listening. Although the effect does not last, it can be reactivated at any time. When music runs counter to our own natural frequency rhythms, however, we can feel irritated and stressed. (Some people find that heavy metal music runs counter to their natural rhythms, others find that new age music does. It's not the type of music that matters—it's the combination of music with personality.)

Follow-up studies suggest that musical rhythm is the critical ingredient for improving performance on spatial tasks. (Performance on other tasks might be affected by tone, melody or volume.) The best way to find out for sure will be through action research. In general, use instrumental music if students will be talking during the music. Use music with words for transitions or setting up an activity.

Suggestions

✔ Play positive, energizing music, such as movie themes, before the start of class.

✔ Play triumphal music, like *The Hallelujah Chorus* or the theme from *Rocky*, to supplement moments of emotional highs.

✔ Play Romantic or Classical music selections behind dramatic prose or for choral reading activities. Baroque music (like Handel's *Water Music* or Vivaldi's *Four Seasons*) played quietly in the background can soothe, calm and relax your group.

✔ Try a Mozart piano sonata before students perform tasks that require spatial-temporal reasoning (like assembling objects, using building blocks or completing puzzles).

✔ Play lyrically appropriate music selections as you conclude your class (like Jennifer Warnes and Bill Medley's *I've Had the Time of My Life* or *Happy Trails* by Dale Evans).

Break the Monotony with Novelty and Fun

We all like predictability in our lives. If we can rely on something good happening, our cortisol and stress levels drop. If we are faced with mild stress (like an impending deadline), cortisol levels rise and spur us into action. Good teaching provides learners with a little bit of each by bringing the excitement of a roller coaster's highs and lows into the day.

Suggestions

✔ **Humor break:** Have everyone stand up and close their eyes. Anyone who can think of a recent or old joke should raise his hand. Tell everyone to open their eyes and, if they do not have their hand raised, cluster around a person who does. The person with the raised hand tells the joke and the audience applauds. Then, have the joke listeners find another joke teller. If a joke listener thinks of a joke in the meantime, she can raise a hand in the next round.

✔ **A new place in space:** At some point during each class day, change seats. Change them to music (in Musical Chairs fashion), rotate by quadrant or just ask students to change places with a classmate—whatever works! Or, ask your class to change the layout of the room so that all the furniture faces a new direction with a different wall as the front of the room.

✔ **Take on new roles:** Have students adopt different personas for fifteen minutes. Choose personalities from history, literature, the sciences or the arts—whatever best fits the day's topic. Have a box of character props (hats, scarves, canes, briefcases, et cetera) on hand for this purpose. Give learners two minutes to get into character and then have them introduce themselves to a partner. Continue the lesson, incorporating student characters into it as much as possible.

Which ideas did I try today? What were the results?
What will I do differently next time?

_____

_____

_____

March the Brain to Learning Success

One of the quickest ways to improve blood circulation and mental focus is with short marching activities. Without a coherent purpose for marching, however, students might be skeptical about its worth. Before telling anyone they are about to march, explain that you are going to conduct a review of what they have learned so far. Prep them with what material you are going to review and then ask them to stand. When they are on their feet, jump right into the activity and have fun!

Marching comes with plenty of fringe benefits. Its very rhythm can enhance learning and what students learn while they are marching is more likely to be remembered later because 1) marching adds a kinesthetic element to learning, 2) sounds and rhymes are catchy and easy to remember, 3) a change of location triggers spatial-episodic memory and 4) it stimulates the senses in a fresh, visceral way. Here are a few variations to try:

Suggestions

✔ **Military march:** Put students into groups so they can march and chant to a steady rhythm in a line like military recruits do. Start with a basic chorus that encapsulates the topic of your lesson or course, like, "This stuff isn't hard to get…wait and see, you'll learn it yet." Before the march, assign the task of coming up with content review/call-response verses to use during the march. Start the class off with a few repeats of the chorus, then have the teams take turns calling out their verses with everyone repeating it back. Repeat the chorus between every verse. Marching like this is fun and healthy!

✔ **Brain laps:** Send students out to do a quick lap of the entire ground floor or outside perimeter of the building to get their circulation up. During this exercise, they tell ten different people what they think the three most important key words are from the last half-hour of class. Be sure to set ground rules before you begin this activity, addressing noise, courtesy, safety, time and other concerns.

✔ **Follow the Leader:** Put students in teams to brainstorms a topic and send them out for a walk. The team leader will dramatize or say something about the topic content and the team members will follow along and repeat it. Use this activity as a repetition memory game or perception and skills practice.

Add Good Stress, Eliminate Bad Stress

This may surprise you: We learn better in the face of low or moderate stress than when faced with high stress or even no stress at all! Moderately stressed learners are resourceful and resilient lifelong learners. Good stress triggers a rush of adrenaline that prepares learners to rise to the challenge of the occasion, evoking their most efficient alert states. On the other hand, negative stress—provoked by anxiety, learned helplessness or perceived threat—releases an excess of glucocorticoids into your system and can inhibit learning in the present and future. The following suggestions will evoke the right kind of stress in your learners so they will be more likely to enjoy your class and give their best effort.

Suggestions

✔ Ensure that learners have all the resources they need to complete a task; a shortage of materials or time will stress them out or induce helplessness.

✔ Experiment with the number of resources you provide. Too much time, support and access to class tools provokes no stress at all; not enough prevents everyone from finishing the work. Limiting resources is not an exact science so experiment until you find the balance.

✔ Avoid irregular or unbeatable deadlines. Time restraints are one thing—they get the body moving—but impossible or unpredictable deadlines are detrimental.

✔ Schedule relaxation or physical movement as de-stressing strategies—a bit of humor or a quick game relieves stress, too.

✔ Eliminate threats of negative consequences to students. This includes expressions such as, "If you do that one more time, I'll…," or, "Quiet down and get ready to learn…."

✔ Encourage the appropriate expression of emotions. Discussions, journaling, pair sharing and physical action engage emotions and relieve the stress of repressing intense feelings.

✔ Take advantage of school guidance counselors. They can teach the whole class ways to manage stress, give you suggestions for diffusing stress within the classroom and counsel particular students undergoing significant stress in their lives.

Playing Games Grows Brains

Teachers encourage cognitive growth and development but students work on social skills at school, too. Many childhood games meet all three objectives at the same time. Books and web sites are full of games to play in the classroom; the following list is just a sampling of things to try.

Suggestions

✔ **Hook and linking games** require players to match words to definitions or identify opposites or similar pairs. Have fun with pictogram games like *Pictionary* or word completion games like *Scrabble*. Or, try seek-and-find games like *Concentration*, I Spy or What's Missing from this Picture?

✔ **Listening games,** like Simon Says, Telephone or reciting tongue twisters, involve hearing and repeating something; students always benefit from practicing auditory skills.

✔ **What am I?** Write keys item for review (like a name, concept or a place) on pieces of paper, one item per page. When students enter your classroom in the morning or after a break, tape a page to each person's back. Students wander around the room asking each person one yes or no question to determine what item they are wearing.

✔ **Word puzzles:** Select several dozen common expressions and phrases (content-related or from the general culture) and format them in a graphic, unusual way; have students work in pairs to solve them. Or, give students a list of these phrases and have them create puzzles out of them. Three examples are presented below to help you get started.

intelligences	eggs	everything
intelligences	easy	pizza
intelligences		
(multiple intelligences)	*(eggs over easy)*	*(pizza with everything on it)*

Which ideas did I try today? What were the results? What will I do differently next time?

_____

_____

_____

The Cycle of Learning

Learners can pay attention to your instruction or sit quietly and create meaning out of it, but they cannot do both at the same time. The human brain does not learn continuously. Design presentations to alternate between focus learning and diffusion. Focus learning is continued, directed attention with minimal learner choice (like listening to a lecture or participating in a group discussion). Diffusion is unfocused time for the learner to choose which concepts and facts to ponder (like journaling, talking with a partner, working on a creative project or just sitting quietly and thinking).

Concurrently, the brain's attention and learning cycle alternates between internal and external awareness. It will focus externally to absorb new information but then turn inward to access memories and associations of events related to that information and generate meaning from it.

Suggestions

✔ Alternate direct instruction time (focus) with discussion, reflection or writing time (diffusion). Cycle between focus and diffusion according to the age of the learner. (For example, direct the learning of ten-year-olds for about ten minutes.) Twenty minutes is the maximum amount of time you should ever require focused learning, even with adults. With any age group, allow about two to five minutes to diffuse new information before returning to your lecture or presentation.

✔ Schedule several minutes of time for purposeful reflection throughout the day. Give learners complete freedom to reflect in any format: writing in a journal, creating a mind map, silently reflecting or drawing.

✔ Take advantage of natural breaks in your schedule for recess, lunch or the end of   the day. Plan your teaching so that complex or detail-heavy instruction falls before one of these breaks to give students extra time to process it after diffusing it in the classroom.

✔ If you see and hear that the group is losing focus and becoming distracted (glazed expressions, wiggling and fidgeting in the seats or minor outbreaks of disruptive behavior), move into a diffusion activity rather than reprimanding them.

Motor Brain Activators

Many early motor skills influence later cognitive skills. For example, walking along a line and balancing on a beam improve vestibular development and spatial skills, which contribute to the development of reading skills. Playing tag practices prediction and theory of mind (what is that person thinking?). Try the following activities with your youngest students, from pre-school through third grade. Each one takes less than five minutes to perform and requires only about twenty minutes of your day. The benefits will accumulate throughout the entire school year.

Liability and safety concerns have all but banished seesaws and merry-go-rounds from playgrounds, even though these fixtures add an essential element of physicality to learning. Fortunately, you can bring elements of this equipment into your classroom.

Suggestions

✔ To give students the chance to jump and use the large muscles of their legs, play "grape-stomping" or hopscotch games.
✔ To provide students the opportunity to fine-tune their spatial orientation, play a game of Triangle Tag instead of lamenting the loss of a merry-go-round. Put students in groups of four. Three people hold hands and run in a circle and the fourth person tries to tag a designated group member while the spinning group turns and changes directions to evade him.
✔ Practice balance with line and beam walking. Students walk at least ten feet along a line that has been painted or taped on the floor (or along a long two-by-four on the ground). Make it harder by having students walk along the line with their eyes closed.

Which ideas did I try today? What were the results?
What will I do differently next time?

_____

_____

_____

Reinforcement and the Brain

Our brains have complex reward systems with lots of conditions for responses and even more exceptions to those conditions. That said, however, there are still reliable ways to improve learning by engaging in rewards. In the early phase of the learning process, consistently give praise so learners get used to it; as the process continues, switch to intermittent praise so they don't become dependent on it. Second, be careful how you word praise. Comments like, "Marina, you've done well at math all year. What's the answer to this question?" can cause anxiety and make learners too nervous to perform. Finally, build reward into tasks and make students the primary source of praise to each other (so you, the teacher, don't have sole responsibility). Competition, peer editing and cooperative problem solving are just a few of the activities with built-in opportunities for feedback and congratulations. If more people are involved in the rewards process, more people benefit from it individually.

Suggestions

✔ Allow learners to help determine the criteria used for assessment. After an assignment, have students assess themselves according to these standards before you say a word. Then, ask the students how they felt about their performance. Finally, contribute your personal opinion about a student's performance in relation to the self-assessment he or she has already outlined to you.
✔ Make sure that any positive feedback you give is specific and immediate.
✔ Provide opportunities for students to generate and give praise (specific, positive, immediate feedback) to each other. Handshakes, notes and team cheers vary this usually verbal activity.
✔ Teach students how to give feedback in a way that respects personal feelings. Model the difference between comments that address a person's work ("You made great eye contact with the audience") and those that refer only to the person ("You're very good at giving oral presentations").

Strengthen Learning with Reviews

New information reaches the brain every minute, very little related to academic content. Teachers should not assume that student brains process and store everything important from a course, nor should they assume that student brains store new knowledge correctly. If what you taught the previous day is important for students to remember, take a few minutes today to review it. Revisiting a topic (however briefly) reminds students that they possess information, allows them to check what is fact against what their brains have stored and emphasizes which concepts are important. Schedule daily reviews.

Suggestions

✔ **Mind maps:** In groups of three or four, students create a mind map of the previous day's learning. Then, they will separate, walk around the room looking at other mind maps, find an idea that they forgot about and return to add that idea to their own maps.

✔ **Frisbee review:** Stand in a circle and toss a Frisbee (or some other object). Whoever catches it recites one thing that he learned during the last class session or connects one thing from the last lesson to another idea or concept.

✔ **Stand-up reviews:** Conduct a content review while everyone is standing. There are many ways you could do this: have students close their eyes, play music, put them in motion, assign a pair-share task or play a fast-paced word association game (one partner says a word from the previous material and the other partner blurts out the first word that comes to mind on that topic).

✔ **I Did It My Way:** Write out the lyrics to a popular song and distribute them to students, who are assigned the task of rewriting the lyrics using key terms and concepts from a previous lesson. Or, rewrite the lyrics as a large group activity and display them on a transparency for everyone to sing aloud together.

Which ideas did I try today? What were the results? What will I do differently next time?

_____

_____

_____

Non-Conscious Messages Are Powerful

Did you know that more than 99 percent of all learning happens at the non-conscious level and only 38 percent of a spoken message is transmitted by words? The conscious mind can process just one sense at a time but the unconscious mind receives many messages per second. Learners pick up much more information than you put into the lesson plan—and they may not even know it. The brain consciously processes only one sensory input signal at a time (like seeing something on the board or hearing a sentence in a lecture) but it unconsciously receives messages from your vocal intonation, gestures and facial expressions. Pay attention to your presentation style to ensure that the message in your mind is the message you send to learners.

Suggestions

✔ Purposely use tonal shifts, change your voice pace and volume and employ gestures to add impact and drama to your presentation style.

✔ Practice your opening greeting in front of a mirror until your face and hands enhance (rather than undermine) your words.

✔ Video record your next presentation. Afterwards, watch and analyze your performance and find three things to learn from it.

✔ Give students forms for written feedback on your delivery style. Include questions about your "soft skills," such as, "How often did the teacher smile at me?"

✔ Call on participants with an outstretched hand with the palm facing up. This gesture is much more inclusive and welcoming than pointing your finger at their face.

✔ Smile and thank students for their participation and specific contributions.

Which ideas did I try today? What were the results? What will I do differently next time?

_____

_____

_____

Gender and Learning Cycles

Students learn at an uneven pace throughout the day. Our internal clock determines the balance of chemicals—testosterone, estrogen, cortisol and a host of other hormones, peptides and neurotransmitters—in our system, all of which influence cognition. Research suggests that the performance of the left hemisphere of the brain increases as testosterone levels decline whereas the performance of the right hemisphere of the brain increases as estrogen levels decline. It is known that the menstrual cycle affects the performance of spatial, verbal and even mental arithmetic tasks. Other findings suggest that higher levels of estrogen may facilitate the automatic activation of verbal representations in memory. Levels of testosterone vary from fifteen to fifty percent over the course of a week; estrogen levels may vary by five hundred percent during the month! Naturally, these fluctuations contribute to significant variations in student achievement on any given day.

Males perform better on spatial and gross motor skills in the morning; females do better on verbal and writing skills during this time. The afternoon reverses these results for both sexes. Midday may be best for rote, repetitive learning for everyone. Afternoons and evening are better for establishing and developing relationships and discovering a more global understanding of the day's new knowledge and events.

Suggestions

✔ Rotate the scheduled time of tasks that are highly verbal or highly spatial. For example, do reading in the morning three days a week and in the afternoon two days week. Likewise, rotate your content delivery so that sometimes you spend the morning learning new or complex concepts and other times reviewing or reciting facts.

✔ Provide choice as to when certain tasks can be done. For example, assign two tasks but give students the option of which one they want to do now and which one later.

✔ Review class material on a daily basis to help students who had trouble understanding it the day before.

✔ Use the end of the day to reflect on new learning. Schedule more social grouping activities at this time—peer interaction will also help wake up sluggish students.

Active Learning III

Early motor development leads to later cognitive development. The brain and motor areas benefit from repetitious, multimodal activities that link visual, auditory, spatial and tactile skills. Here is another list of motor activities for your youngest students, from pre-school through third grade. Each one takes less than five minutes to perform and requires only about twenty minutes of your day. The benefits will accumulate throughout the entire school year.

Suggestions

✔ **Tracing activities** develop kinesthetic and spatial awareness skills. Have students locate a picture and trace it, first from the original and then from their tracing. Or, have them trace only the outlines and fill in the details freehand.

✔ **Swinging and rocking** stimulate the vestibular system and develop the inner ear, balance and reading skills. Swings and slides, however, are increasingly hard to find on playgrounds. Ask a special education teacher or occupational therapist for sensory tools to use inside the classroom, like a balance board or a rocker board. Or, devise alternatives. For example, place a board about two feet long and one foot wide on a dowel or roller (like a rolling pin) and have students try to balance themselves on it (with the support of a wall or chair, if necessary).

✔ **Spinning** develops the brain. Play loud, upbeat music and have students spin in a circle (in one direction) with their eyes closed (they'll be less dizzy and get more practice orienting themselves). Then, switch directions. Spin twice a day for one minute in each direction.

✔ **Hopping, clapping and skipping:** Lead the class in a hop-clap rhythm until they learn the pattern. As they become more confident, ask student volunteers to lead the pattern or choreograph their own. Incorporate these types of games into your schedule at least once a week.

✔ **Stirring, winding and groove boards**: Stirring and winding motions encourage better spatial perceptual skills. Spend a class making no-bake cookies, letting each child stir the batter. Bring in colorful yarn and have them wind it on a spool; have students use sticks of varying lengths (longer is harder) to follow a grooved path in a flat board.

Curriculum and the Developing Brain

Even with curricular mandates, you have full control over how to present material to students. Meet the needs of your students' brains with proactively meaningful content. The brain balances self-identity, security and safety with exploration and novelty from the ages of four to seven (with individual exceptions, of course). From the ages of seven to eleven, students are concerned with making friends, achieving competency at different things and observing (and commenting on) bodily functions. During early adolescence, the brain focuses on improving social status, finding peer approval, taking risks and exploring sexuality. From late adolescence through early adulthood (up to the age of twenty-five), the brain is interested in independence, attracting a mate and securing social and financial survival. If you can incorporate any of these issues into your lessons, you will have far more success capturing students' attention and making learning meaningful.

Suggestions

✔ Acknowledge these developmental stages and work with (rather than against) students as they go through them. For example, support the desire to socialize with cooperative learning, teams and paired work projects. Support the interest with bodily functions by adding "gross out" factors to lessons and worksheets.

✔ Hang posters and examples of student heroes that reflect age-appropriate developmental values. By the age of fifteen, students can choose their own role models and work together as teams to create a large montage for display.

✔ Establish learning centers and give students time to visit them so they can pursue subjects that interest them personally.

✔ Give students more control over their own learning. Select unit or weekly themes according to what learners feel they need to learn, such as social contact skills, developing autonomy, finding personal security, making money, pleasing others or identifying and fulfilling ambitions.

Which ideas did I try today? What were the results?
What will I do differently next time?

_____

_____

_____

Schedule Brain Breaks!

The brain is not designed for continuous input. It needs time for reflection, consolidation and integration. Sometimes the best learning happens away from formal instruction, with an insight or inspiration. Here are a few activities that give the brain a break and free it to make discoveries.

Suggestions

✔ **Writing your name with body parts:** Have students stand up and "write" their first name with their elbow, their middle name with their other elbow, their last name with their hip, their best friend's name with their other hip and a parent's name with their head.

✔ **Stretching:** Invite a student to lead a series of stretches. This leader sets the pace (slow, relaxing movements or calisthenics) and chooses any accompanying music. Rotate the role of leader. Students can stretch as one large group or in smaller teams of four or five people, with one leader at each.

✔ **Body measuring:** Student pairs get three minutes to measure something in the room with some part of their bodies. Their goal is to invent the most creative unit of measure. After the deadline has passed, the pairs report their result to the rest of the group their results: This cabinet is 210 knuckles long.

✔ **Opposites attract:** Without speaking, one student partner touches an object in the room and the other partner—still without speaking—touches either a similar object or an opposite object. Give the pairs one minute to touch five object pairs, taking turns going first.

Which ideas did I try today? What were the results? What will I do differently next time?

_____

_____

_____

Replace Rewards and Bribes with Desire

A reward is any predictable consequence that has market value to the learner: "Perform A and you'll get B." Used often with (so-called) unmotivated learners and low achievers, rewards carry with them such unwanted side effects as the reduction of intrinsic motivation and a cap on achievement. They encourage a predictable behavior but ultimately negate the joy of learning. Rewards also impair higher-order thinking skills and reduce contextual memory.

The brain is naturally motivated; learning is a survival instinct. The more we use tokens, bribes, coupons and rewards to generate learning, though, the more we condition intrinsic motivation out of the system and ruin the pleasure of learning. An old model of teaching was a behaviorist one: choose the behavior you want from students and reward them for doing it. A new model—inspiring your students to learn naturally, without bribes or coercion—works far better than controlling, manipulative, brain-antagonistic approaches.

Suggestions

✔ Stop bribing and rewarding your learners. Phase out existing bribes and rewards over time.

✔ Model your own joy and love for learning so students understand that you seek knowledge for its own sake, not for some extrinsic reward.

✔ Allow learners more choice and control in their learning to enhance their intrinsic motivation.

✔ Increase the quantity and quality of feedback to give students needed reinforcement without material rewards. Have students develop ways to acknowledge each other. They can personalize variations of the high five, make up chants and cheers and devise other ways to congratulate another person's work.

✔ Celebration milestones and acknowledge accomplishment to embed the value of learning in individuals and the entire group.

Which ideas did I try today? What were the results?
What will I do differently next time?

_____

_____

_____

Discipline Strategies that Make Sense

There are specific, practical solutions for reducing the likelihood of discipline problems and there are specific ways to successfully address them if they do occur. The following strategies are based on two important concepts. First, spatial memory links each experience with a location. Therefore, criticism, embarrassments and putdowns will be forever associated with you or your classroom. Avoid them. Second, all brain-body behaviors are dependent on mental states. Keep learners in a good brain state for learning and change them out of bad states if they enter them.

Suggestions

✔ Employ positive relationships, emotions, challenge and novelty during the process of learning to hold learner focus. The use of student teams and team leaders make learning more intimate; revolving leadership challenges individuals and prevents group dynamics from becoming stale.

✔ Change activities whenever student behavior becomes inappropriate. Don't address issues—just change. Engage a different type of intelligence, alter your tone of voice, speak from a different place in the room, turn off the lights or stand everyone up for a stretch break.

✔ Manage learners' mental states, not specific behaviors. Behaviors are spontaneous and unpredictable; in comparison, activating a sense of anticipation or pleasure for an upcoming activity takes less effort and requires less maintenance. If learners are not in the right "mood" for a particular activity (like a quiet, studious one), spend a few minutes putting them there (with deep breathing or peaceful music in the background). That way, you won't have to fight for their attention.

✔ Move to a corner or "hot spot" of the room when heavy discipline is necessary. Never be stern from the front of the room; you'll contaminate that area (probably your primary content-delivery area) with bad associations. Always give the same warning and consequences as part of your discipline strategy.

✔ Outline examples of better behavior with specific storytelling and metaphors about the power of silence or restraint.

The Chemistry of Choice

We know that choice changes the chemistry and behavior of the brain. But how does it do so? When learners are given the opportunity to choose their task, resources or parameters for accomplishment, their stress is lower. They feel more positive about the task and look forward to participating and (hopefully) succeeding at it. This enthusiasm triggers the release of "optimal thinking" brain chemicals. (The two neurotransmitters that trigger confidence seem to be dopamine and serotonin.)

On the other hand, when we feel hopeless or depressed or that we lack the power to make choices, the brain has a different chemical reaction. In this case, it produces norepinephrine, a neurotransmitter with a strong inhibiting effect. In this brain state, morale is low, learning is inefficient and motivation is weak. Brain chemistry changes and outward states influence each other, positively or negatively.

Suggestions

✔ Soften directive, controlling words ("You'll see that…" and "You'll learn…") by interspersing them with expressions that offer choice ("You might like to…," "You may find that…," or, "Others have found….")

✔ Allow your learners to continually make appropriate choices for their learning. Give them a menu of acceptable learning topics or let them devise their own. Vary the type and amount of choice you offer according to the age of your learners or the applicability of the subject. Realize, too, that an excess of choice will drive learners towards topics with which they are already familiar. Too little choice, however, and they'll never develop a passion for learning.

✔ Give learners input on the criteria you'll use to assess them.

Which ideas did I try today? What were the results? What will I do differently next time?

_____

_____

_____

Hollywood, Here I Come!

These role-playing activities involve kinesthetic, spatial, verbal and linguistic elements, as well as engage emotions and build problem-solving skills.

Suggestions

✔ **Expert interviews:** One member of a student pair poses as an expert on a topic; the other partner poses as a crack reporter. Allow ten minutes for the experts to brush up on facts and the reporters to write questions on key issues. Then, put students in their pairs to conduct and give interviews. Have them switch roles for five minutes. Finally, bring the whole group back together to debrief. Make this activity as dramatic as possible with costumes or music.

✔ **Retro party:** Identify an historical era that provides a context for your new lesson (like the early 1900s—when Marie Curie discovered radium—for a lesson about nuclear energy or the late 1700s for your study of the U. S. Constitution). Brainstorm ways life might have been different then (considering dress, language, manners, opportunity and personal freedom). Then, have everyone stand up, close their eyes and imagine themselves traveling twenty, three hundred or one thousand years back in time into this era. Lead a discussion with the entire group on topics that people from that time would be interested in, especially as it relates to the subject you are about to study. Finally, identify objects in the room that would have been around at that time.

✔ **All the world's a stage:** Unexpectedly pause during your next lecture and have students stand up and form small groups of three to five people. Assign the groups the task of turning something from the last hour of lecture, learning or discussion into a three-minute skit. During science, students could perform a dialogue between the sun, planets, debris and comets of the solar system; creative students might act out a discipline policy you reminded them of during silent reading time. Other topics could include dramatizing a famous meeting between two historical figures or discussing the merits of the book they are reading for English.

Which ideas did I try today? What were the results? What will I do differently next time?

_____

_____

_____

Reduce Common Forms of Perceived Threat

Our brain is strongly influenced by four enemies of learning: threat, excessive stress, anxiety and induced learner helplessness. Each of these menaces causes the brain to shut itself down to minimal performance; at minimal performance, you use less of your brain to learn and revert to stored, reactive behaviors. Threats also reduce higher-order thinking skills and creativity, and diminish memory. Statements as seemingly innocent as, "I'll just stand here and wait until you quiet down," can be perceived as threatening; a learner who cannot see or hear directions very well (perhaps because of seat placement) might feel anxious. Nearly anything can induce learner helplessness, from forgetting a textbook at home, to lacking resources necessary to complete an assignment. Although educators are quick to notice when students fail to participate fully or when student performance is not up to standard, they are not often able to recognize when they are the ones creating a climate of threat that intimidates the class.

Suggestions

✔ Avoid academic surprises like pop quizzes. Continually reassure the learners of the likelihood of their success.

✔ Establish a climate in which learners feel comfortable making mistakes—we learn best from mistakes! Don't be afraid to point out your own mistakes and how they strengthen knowledge and wisdom. As a class, invent a silly cheer to turn bloopers into a funny ritual.

✔ Provide plenty of wait time after asking questions so students don't feel pressured to have the correct answer immediately. Establish a sense of social safety by answering every student question completely and pleasantly.

✔ Avoid intimidating discipline tactics. If you have to point out a mistake or reprimand a student, do it in private and offer constructive advice for the future.

✔ Provide time for learners time to de-stress upon arrival in your class; lead stretching routines, conduct personal discussions, play music or assign journaling and reflection tasks.

✔ Never use staying beyond the close of class as a threat to learners.

✔ Never allow students to put each other down.

Increase "By-Product" Learning

Kids playing and inventing games in the neighborhood park learn more than just formal rules—they informally learn camaraderie, cooperation, negotiation and physical skills. These informal fringe benefits are known as "by-product" learning because they occur as part of another process.

The more often you can engage by-product learning, the less didactic and heavy-handed your instruction style will be. A group of kindergartners working in a cooperative group to write a story learn collaborative skills as they learn to write. Adolescents spending a math class buying and remodeling an imaginary house also learn negotiation and research skills, practice using percentages and measurements and are exposed to concepts that involve money and banking.

Suggestions

✔ Discover what activities interest your students and design content lessons around them.

✔ Use outdoor games to build teamwork, self-confidence and trust.

✔ Devise large, multi-disciplinary projects that require students to utilize many resources and learn new skills to complete. Publish a class yearbook, create a welcome guide for new students or research, write and illustrate a class encyclopedia on a topic from the curriculum, like ecology or American history.

✔ Establish cooperative learning groups to increase opportunities to share and build knowledge.

✔ Watch snippets of videos and discuss how to learn from them. Have students write reviews and draw conclusions from the programs to apply in real life.

✔ Give students an assignment to perform the next time they visit a public place, like a shopping mall or restaurant, or when they ride the bus home from school. The next school day, have them work with partners to share the results of what they learned or observed.

Which ideas did I try today? What were the results? What will I do differently next time?

_____

_____

_____

Learning with Both Sides of the Brain

Everyone knows that the left side of the brain is an expert at logic, order and reason and that the right side specializes in creativity, emotions and music. At least, everyone thinks they know that... is it true? To the extent that some of us prefer to think sequentially and others prefer to approach problems with non-linear strategies, yes, but these preferences neither define nor limit our abilities. Neuroscientists now know that we engage both sides of the brain during nearly every activity—they are spheres of specialization rather than exclusivity. (Edward De Bono's work on lateral thinking revealed that the left brain can be the creative side. Musicians process music in the left hemisphere of the brain more than non-musicians do.) The following suggestions explore ways to appeal to both sides of your students' brains.

Suggestions

✔ Open every new topic by presenting the big picture of the entire unit, verbally through lecture and discussion and visually with video and graphic organizers (like hierarchical trees).

✔ Give students a list or outline of everything you plan to cover in a lesson, topic or unit. Provide either one giant list that covers everything (it would also help learners organize their notes) or smaller, detailed ones each day.

✔ Hang posters and peripherals relevant to the whole unit so that learners always have a global map of the material close at hand.

✔ Incorporate music, drama and physical movement as much as possible.

✔ Always alert students when you are about to present information that is critical or very important. (You'll still have plenty of room in your presentation for spontaneity.)

✔ Before, during and at the conclusion of any lesson, encourage learners to map out and describe on paper their understanding of the topic. At the end of the week, give students several options of graphic organizers to use and tell them refer to class notes and textbooks as they map out a week's worth of content. Collect the student work—it gives you immediate information about what they learned and forgot—and use it to identify what holes you need to fill in on Monday.

Grow Out, Not Fill Up

Filling students' brains with knowledge by planning every last detail of their content instruction is going about it the wrong way. Brain-friendly teachers plan for learning by helping students branch out from knowledge they already have, extending the knowledge, reframing it or presenting it in a new context. This approach is student-centered, learner-compatible and very user-friendly.

Learners have no way of knowing the details, emotional attachment and depth of meaning that you have as an instructor. The only meaningful starting point for student learning is what they already know. Consider the following suggestions when you plan your next unit:

Suggestions

✔ **Preparation:** Activate prior knowledge, create immersion environments, help students set learning goals and wake up learning brains with cross-lateral movements and relaxing stretches. Always express strong, positive expectations for your students' performance.

✔ **Globalization:** Move from concrete experience to the abstract—never the opposite. Providing context and presenting a global overview of the information you intend to cover are critical initial strategies.

✔ **Initiation:** Give students real-life problems to solve, take field trips, interview experts in the field (or people who actually witnessed an historical event) and design lots of hands-on learning.

✔ **Elaboration:** Have students think about the topic, write about the topic, ask thoughtful questions, research databases, write tests, conduct peer discussions and design graphic organizers to approach the material in lots of different ways.

✔ **Incubation:** Let new knowledge incubate. Schedule down time for the brain, allow for unguided reflection in journals, discussions or artwork, take a recess break or take a day off from the content altogether.

✔ **Verification:** Give students the chance to formally demonstrate what they know by taking tests that they write themselves, assessing themselves according to standards they helped draft or informally participating in small group discussions or playing cooperative games.

✔ **Celebration:** Celebrate important successes or learning milestones with peer reinforcement, high fives, class cheers and individual acknowledgment.

Learning Is Messy

Learning occurs across multiple pathways that are conducting simultaneous inputs. Our brains process sights, sounds, smells, tastes and tactile sensations all at once. Experiences that engage all of the physical senses—walking through a museum or down the street, visiting a foreign country, attending a concert, listening to a guest speaker, going to a sporting event or trying something completely new—grow lots of dendrites (the connections between brain cells) and enhance learning by association. Although linear lesson plans with a sequential, single sensory input approach will induce learning, they stimulate very little else. Anyway, once you're immersed in learning, the path takes unexpected turns. Keep your guides, overviews, previews and graphic organizers (students need a sense of structure and a path to follow) but open up your instruction to opportunities that engage the senses.

Suggestions

✔ Establish learning centers that engage multiple senses. Whenever possible, bring students to other rooms on campus or locations off campus so they can learn in a new environment. For example, visit the cafeteria kitchen to learn about nutrition or a local medical clinic to learn about viruses.

✔ Include audiovisual components, active movement or scents and fragrances in your lesson plans; add activities that appeal to each of the different learning styles.

✔ Raise your tolerance for discussion noise—partner, group and teamwork activities will make your room louder.

✔ Split your classroom into two littler ones. In one half of the room, you teach to one half of your students; in the other half of the room, they work in groups or in pairs to teach each other. This will give each student the chance to become personally involved in the learning process.

Which ideas did I try today? What were the results? What will I do differently next time?

_____

_____

_____

Trigger Learning

Most of what the brain learns cannot be easily measured with current assessment tools. Even neuroscientists have a hard time identifying exactly how learning occurs. We have a good understanding of learning at the cellular level but in the classroom environment it is far more complex. Is learning a behavior change? Is it a change of opinion? Is it a feeling? Do "street smarts" count? These questions are not readily answered. Fortunately, there are several steps you can take to ensure that your students actually learn what you present; following these suggestions will make any later assessment more indicative.

Suggestions

✔ Ask students to explain, discuss, build on and demonstrate their academic, intellectual and psychological knowledge of a subject; pose to them thought-provoking questions like, "Where do you think all this rain is coming from?" Inquire how they know what they know by asking questions like, "How did you figure out this problem?" Allow them to demonstrate their knowledge visually with flow charts or by drawing if they prefer not to verbally explain it.

✔ Ask students to calculate their personal bias for or against the material. Have them rate different elements of a subject on a scale of one to ten, both before and after they learn it. Realize that passion is contagious—if you feel strongly (one way or another) about what you teach, students will probably, too.

✔ Constantly teach interdisciplinary aspects of your subject. How can you use math in geology? What does health science have to do with history? Survey students to find out how they might use the knowledge of one field in another. Discuss how learning affects the real lives of your students, their community or the rest of the world.

✔ Begin every new lesson by tying it to some example of personal relevance. Once you've demonstrated that what students are about to learn really matters, you can move on to more abstract, academic applications.

Which ideas did I try today? What were the results?
What will I do differently next time?

_____

_____

_____

Groups Are OK, Labels Are Not

You should reject the practice of labeling learners by ability for several reasons: 1) Labeling low-performing learners often contributes to a self-fulfilling prophecy of failure. 2) Learners may excel at skills other than the ones you are teaching or using for assessment. 3) Negative labels imply that learners are somehow deficient or damaged, even though they bring years of life experience to your class or presentation—the human brain can't help but learn! 4) Previous teachers who assigned such labels may have been unable to tap into these learners' abilities. 5) Assessment models are insufficient to measure all ranges of success. 6) The brain of a learner, especially a younger learner, may be developing more slowly, albeit still normally, than the brains of peers. 7) School performance is a very poor predictor of future greatness—many famous people labeled "slow" or "average" went on to make astounding contributions to society.

Suggestions

✔ Build flexibility into ability grouping. Just because a student begins in one group does not mean that he or she will always belong there.

✔ Avoid references not just to "slow" learners but also to "fast" or "smart" learners.

✔ Design learning centers to appeal to multiple intelligences and different styles of learning.

✔ Use student interests and backgrounds as the source for new learning. Skill at basketball can be turned into a reason to study math (in order to calculate player or team statistics). Students who claim they are motivated only by money may enjoy economics as a means to gain knowledge about amassing and expanding future wealth.

Which ideas did I try today? What were the results? What will I do differently next time?

_____

_____

_____

Don't Trigger Helpless Learning States

Past traumatic classroom experiences can resurface and trigger states of learner helplessness that leave students feeling overwhelmed, anxious or resigned. Often, students experiencing such feelings of helplessness give up and refuse to try, even when there are sufficient resources available to complete a project or task. Traumatic classroom experiences usually involve a student's perception of intense threat and stress in the face of uncontrollable circumstances; imagine a student who does not read very well being told to read aloud an entire paragraph in front of the whole class. Once an event like that is firmly entrenched in a student's memory, even a mildly threatening situation can trigger helplessness later.

Once students have become immobilized by threat, it will take time to desensitize them by giving them opportunity to make lots of positive, controlled learning choices. Lab experiments suggest that students with induced helplessness may require up to fifty attempts (with plenty of positive reinforcement) to choose a better approach to learning the next time they feel threatened by a task or assignment. Teachers who give up on students after only five attempts may erroneously label them as unmotivated or obstinate. Be patient—it takes time to break the cycle of learned helplessness.

Suggestions

✔ Before beginning or continuing a lesson, solicit feedback from students to find out what they already know or need to know to understand the rest. Ask for a show of hands or thumbs-up, distribute a written questionnaire, observe students at work or ask to see a history of what the class has already studied in order to garner this information.

✔ Clearly identify both available and unavailable resources before beginning a task so students know exactly what they have to work with and which approaches to avoid.

✔ Allow partner or team collaboration on projects and assignments for at least half of your instructional time. It fosters a supportive learning environment.

✔ Give directions slowly and repeat them when necessary. If possible, state the directions orally and present them visually. Have students repeat directions back to you or to a neighbor.

Welcome to Center Stage!

The brain stores memories in our body and mind and locates them by context. We retrieve those stored memories from both spatial cues and content cues. The more a classroom drama or role-playing activity mimics the physiological and psychological states students enter to when they apply the information in real life, the better they will be able to retrieve the memory of learning it when they need it later.

Several positive things happen when your learners engage in role-play. First, they are more motivated to fully participate. Second, enthusiasm for a subject greatly enhances their ability to remember it. Third, physically acting out a concept stores the memory not just in the mind but also in the body (from the feel of the motion to the sound of the words). Finally, working in groups allows students to learn from and teach each other, which will not only help them understand exactly how much content knowledge they already have but also provides informal feedback on their performance.

Suggestions

✔ Let students script and choreograph their own skits, reenactments or presentations within a broad topic or theme that you assign.

✔ Use role-playing strategies that are as close to real-life skills, ideas, information and applications as possible. For example, ask students to role play being rebuffed by a fellow classmate, making friends in a new neighborhood, opening a checking account or enrolling at a driving school.

✔ Motivate learners' excitement and sense of purpose by giving them authentic reasons to participate (team points) or intrinsic reasons to participate (the opportunity to teach a personal skill to others).

✔ Ensure that any competitive games you play have a win-win conclusion so everyone feels safe taking risks during the game and would want to play again.

✔ Establish teams, play music, set deadlines and utilize sound effects. Without these kinds of emotional enhancements, projects are just another form of busy work and tedium.

Simon Says Lives Again

Although most students can hear without any problems, listening skills require practice. A skilled listener can tune into relevant auditory stimulus while filtering out extra sounds and distractions. In an academic world where much content is presented orally, students would benefit from the chance to practice this ability. Dozens of childhood games effectively build learning and listening skills because they combine having fun with increasing knowledge. Incorporate more play into your day. But truly make it play—games can be stressful and some people have bad memories of certain games because of the way they were played when they were children.

So consider this: When I play Simon Says with a group of learners, nobody loses. No one is embarrassed, humiliated or has to sit down and wait out the rest of the game while watching everyone else play. If my participants make a mistake, they keep on playing. They know they've made an error; there is no advantage to pointing it out to the rest of the class. Besides, if everyone stays involved with the game, everyone continues to learn.

Suggestions

✔ **Listening games:** Play Simon Says as a listening game to give smaller children practice following oral instructions.

✔ **Ice-breaker activity:** Help adults warm up to your training and to each other by giving directions like, "Simon says to shake hands and introduce yourself to your neighbor," or, "Simon says to wave at someone you've never met before today."

✔ **Content review:** Use Simon Says to review academic content with instructions: "Simon says to point to the direction of Alaska" (you might need to mark the points of the compass on the walls for this one!). "Simon says to use your body to represent the sum of five and six," "Simon says to point to *tu boca*." "Simon says to point to something in this room that would not have existed one century ago."

Which ideas did I try today? What were the results?
What will I do differently next time?

_____

_____

_____

Finding the Challenges

Utilize the brain's innate tendencies to your advantage. We naturally seek the stimulation that comes from novelty, so use novelty to keep student attention and interest. The introduction of a new idea, unfamiliar food or even wearing a new outfit can all be exciting to learners. On the other hand, the brain also seeks the safety and security of familiarity, so be sure to always balance novelty with episodes of predictability (repetitive, purposeful rituals are one way to do this).

Also, brains love some degree of challenge. Without it, we revert to inertia. With too much, we feel overwhelmed. Find the happy medium, where the degree of challenge matches the learner's skill level and students feel safe to explore and tackle new problems; that is, find the CLD—the correct level of difficulty. Because learners have varying degrees of ability and different levels of expertise, offering cooperative group learning and opportunities to choose assignments can improve your chances of striking the right balance.

Suggestions

✔ Invite learners to participate in the teaching process. Have them plan and present mini-lessons to the rest of the class. This strategy incorporates novelty and challenge.

✔ Vary the amount of resources available to students for different assignments (like the help available, how much initial information you give them and the amount of supplies students can use). To make tasks harder or more complex, set higher completion standards or require a public presentation of new learning. To make them easier, allow more time, let students work in groups or with partners or provide key information about a topic so students don't have to look it up.

✔ Some students will find any assignment too easy or too hard. Monitor those students and their performance on a task and, next time, add an element of challenge (invite them to be a group leader) or remove an element of challenge (let them work with a study buddy or take more time to complete a task).

Stimulate Input, Not Just Output

What one brain finds stimulating may bore another. Occasional novelty in the classroom might be perceived as fun (or stressful!) but consistent novelty is what drives brain reorganization and neural changes. Surprisingly, the brain grows according to the novelty of its input, not by its output (what students express and produce). Novel input reorganizes the brain by reallocating nerve cells to other areas of the brain and stimulating better neuronal connections. When musicians listen to new notes, rhythms or chords, brain cells in their auditory cortex are learning how to listen better the next time music plays. When athletes practice new techniques, their brain cells grow new branches to other cells to perfect the maneuver. In a classroom setting, solving problems is one way to develop the brain. Another means is through purposeful, multi-sensory stimulation.

Suggestions

✔ Expose students to new types of music. Experiment with world music, jazz, drumming, Classical and electronic music.

✔ Ask students to experiment with stretching postures, invent new handshakes or design celebration rituals and novel greetings.

✔ Have students trace strange or foreign objects onto paper and fill in the details.

✔ Interview students about their thoughts while they are working on a project, solving a problem or observing a classroom incident. Record the interview with a tape recorder or have another student take notes. If a student claims to have no thoughts, have him describe his actions to the last detail ("I am holding my pencil at a forty-five degree angle and pressing down lightly as I write the first sentence of my essay."). Describing the obvious is boring—students will lapse into introspection and analysis without even being aware of it if they talk or write long enough.

Which ideas did I try today? What were the results? What will I do differently next time?

_____

_____

_____

The Importance of Beginnings and Endings

One way to wake up the brain is to present it with change. Change signals the brain to pay attention to determine whether what's going on is good or bad. The brain's first response to any information it receives is from the perspective of survival. We exhibit the strongest reactions to beginnings, endings and altered circumstances. It certainly is a useful instinct—we run as fast as we can at the sound of a scary roar and relax when the sound disappears. In the class-room, change triggers the most attentional bias and signals the possibility of something important about to happen. The beginning and ending of any activi-ty opens the window of your students' special attention, so be sure to take advantage of this moment of natural receptiveness to new information!

Suggestions

✔ Start the day with a hook! Provide critical information at the beginning of each class. Spend the first thirty seconds summarizing the key points of that day's lesson or conduct a quick call-response activity to review the content of the previous day.

✔ Develop rituals to handle unwanted interruptions. Where student attention goes, energy goes—you might as well follow it. Teach third-grade students, for example, to turn to the door whenever an unexpected guest drops by and say in unison, "Welcome to Mrs. Peterson's classroom!" Activities like these help everyone process the interruption (all at once) so their brains can forget about it and return to the lesson. (Be consistent with rituals; their power is in their predictability.)

✔ Frequent breaks create more beginnings and endings. Lead students through quick, (thirty seconds) reviews before and after them.

✔ Keep students on their toes with novelty and challenge. Without warning, ask a few individuals to stand and give a one-minute lecture on the day's topic.

✔ Add strong emotional appeal to your class openings and endings with physical activity, music, personal sharing or group celebration.

1...2...3...Switch Jobs!

Are your students a little tired of the sound of your voice? Are you tired of it yourself? Students appreciate change even from the nicest instructors. Guest speakers provide an enriching experience that enhances student memory and recall.

Teachers should take a week to build a class "yellow pages" of all the things students are good at, their parents are good at and members of their community are good at. When the content of your curriculum lends itself to an expert or alternate point of view, ask someone in to present it. You'll have a supply of guest speakers already at your fingertips. Professional association membership directories are additional resources that come to mind. There's no harm in asking your peers to speak to your group. Who knows? They might say yes.

Suggestions

✔ Ask for guest speaker referrals from other teachers, administration or even the PTA.
✔ Invite a teacher from another department to come speak on a topic from a different angle.
✔ Scan the newspapers (don't forget the local independent ones) for community authors, scholars and experts who might be willing to come speak for a few minutes.

Which ideas did I try today? What were the results? What will I do differently next time?

_____

_____

_____

Cycles of Learning

Do your learners claim they are right-brained or left-brained? They are probably both. The brain naturally fluctuates from one hemisphere to the other in ninety-minute cycles over the course of a day. Depending on where they are in they cycle, one hemisphere will have a dominating influence over their thinking and learning. We've all experienced this; you'll be working hard at some extremely linear task and ZAP! Within seconds, you are brain dead and ready for a break. The same sudden shift happens to your students, too.

Learners stuck in the left hemisphere of the brain may complain of trying to solve a problem and finding that each solution path leads to a dead end. Learners stuck in the right brain are much more overwhelmed; they may feel completely lost and have no idea about how to even get started solving the problem. Keep a variety of strategies on hand to awaken student brains by activating both hemispheres. You won't be able to influence the coming and going of hemispheric dominance permanently—it is an innate cycle—but you can affect it in the short term with exercise, nutrition, emotions and cross lateral motion.

Suggestions

✔ Share this information about brain cycles with students so they know how to empower their own learning. Provide more choice of classroom activity so they can switch gears when they tire from pursuing one task, or so they can work on something low-key (like silent reading, notebook review or working on a practice puzzle) when their brain is least effective.

✔ Give students opportunities to move around the classroom. Send them on errands, let them jump rope or even just stand and walk around.

✔ Find a few cross-lateral activities to conduct. March in place while alternating touching the right knee with the left hand and the left knee with the right hand. Without even leaving their seats, students can pat themselves on opposite sides of the back or touch each elbow with the opposite hand.

Which ideas did I try today? What were the results?
What will I do differently next time?

_____

_____

_____

Multiple Strategies for Better Recall

Research suggests that our memories are not stored as images; we recreate them on the spot whenever we want to recall something. There is no memory center in the brain, however; existing memories change as they are altered by our experiences, values, beliefs and biases.

The more variety you can add to new knowledge that learners store in their brains, the more accurate their recollection of it will be. Sights, smells, sounds and touch all contribute to richer, more complex memories than a workbook activity or even multimedia CDs. Even within the most sensory-detailed environment, learners need continual opportunities to share, discuss, reflect on, teach and restate their knowledge to keep it fresh in their minds and develop deeper meaning for it (which further improves retention).

Suggestions

✔ Immediately after teaching new information, have students discuss, draw or act out the material. The following day, have them create a mind map of everything they remember about it and then teach it to a partner.

✔ Conduct weekly discussions about lesson content to help students put the material into perspective. Alternately, have them begin projects or mind maps of the material and add to them each week.

✔ Assign longer tasks that require in-depth comprehension rather than shorter tasks that require students only to regurgitate facts.

✔ At the end of a unit or course, let students summarize what they've learned by building models, producing videos, conducting and transcribing interviews, teaching the class or demonstrating the big picture of what they've learned by representing and analyzing it in some other way.

Which ideas did I try today? What were the results? What will I do differently next time?

_____

_____

_____

Hydration Supports Learning

Much has been written about the role of water in learning. Let's set the record straight: Drinking water does not make you smarter. However, research reveals that dehydration affects performance. The first stage of dehydration is restlessness—thirsty students are antsy and have trouble sitting still. If they aren't able to drink water, they become lethargic (a mechanism that preserves energy) and give up pursuing academic tasks. Have water available for students but avoid going overboard. Insisting that students drink water when they don't need it is silly. In fact, one study showed that dehydrated students perform better after drinking water but hydrated students who drank water when they didn't need it did worse!

Suggestions

✔ Role model drinking water during your class by constantly sipping from a bottle at your desk.

✔ Allow students to keep water in sports bottles at their own desks.

✔ Encourage students to drink water right before class.

✔ Explain to your students about the role of hydration in brain function.

✔ Provide water bottles to students to keep at their desks (or make them part of their school supplies list). Incorporate filling the water bottles into your morning routine.

Which ideas did I try today? What were the results? What will I do differently next time?

_____

_____

_____

The Power of Models and Mapping

What do your students know and how do they know it? Their behavior, participation in discussions and performance on written assignments will provide you glimpses of their "mental maps" of a subject as you teach it. Some maps are sketchy and skeletal, some hierarchically organized and coherent, others distorted and flat-out inaccurate. Find out which students hold what kinds of maps before you begin instruction on a topic so you can develop an instructional approach that corrects misconceptions and expands on prior knowledge. That way, learners can collect and organize new information in a meaningful way. The following activities serve as windows into students' minds and help you customize your teaching strategies to meet everyone's specific needs rather than throwing new information at the class in a "one size fits all" approach.

Suggestions

✔ Before beginning a unit or lesson, review what was learned in the past by making associations in a fun, quick game. Or, have students work together in small groups to create a huge, conceptual graphic organizer of everything they already know about the topic.

✔ Teach your students how to make many different types of graphic organizers, mind maps, tables and diagrams so they can connect and analyze information on their own.

✔ Provide global overviews of a topic before beginning or concluding a unit.

✔ Have students work together in large groups to connect all the information they've learned in a colorful, pictorial way.

✔ Use the information that students have mapped or organized to help you plan your instruction. Find points of commonality between what you planned to teach and what they already know, or erroneous ideas and misconceptions that you could address. Ask students about these bits of knowledge that they have. "Why do you think that…?" and, "Why did you say that…?" are great beginnings for questions that arouse curiosity about the topic.

Why Use Aromas in Learning?

Scientists have been studying the impact of aromas on the brain for years. Smells activate very primitive areas of the brain like the amygdala and thalamus, which respond to danger, pleasure and food. As a result, new smells get high priority in the brain. One section particularly influenced is the limbic area, which is responsible for attention. Everyone knows that the smell of freshly baked bread, cookies or popcorn raises attention and awareness levels dramatically. Why? The sense of smell is processed differently than any other physical sense and enjoys uninterrupted, unfiltered access to the brain. A person can actually react to an aroma before being aware of having inhaled it!

Suggestions

✔ Lemon, cinnamon or peppermint oils affect attention and mood; aromatic flowers can also be effective. Fruit and freshly cut leaves work, too.

✔ Use fans to circulate scent throughout the classroom.

✔ Occasionally introduce new aromas to the group to catch their attention.

✔ Be respectful of those with allergies—not everyone can tolerate heavy scents, even natural ones.

✔ Err on the side of caution—too little scent is better than too much.

✔ Many commercial aromas are produced with very little of the genuine essence. Lavender is the best scent to use if you are relying on manufactured scents.

Which ideas did I try today? What were the results?
What will I do differently next time?

_____

_____

_____

Let the Brain Nibble at New Ideas

Have you ever tried to explain a mind-boggling new concept to someone who just doesn't get it at first? Comprehension lags when learners have no prior information or experience to relate to new ideas. Our understanding of a concept is based in part on the development of past models; new paradigms lack the existing networks that establish understanding. You may understand parts of a new paradigm but probably not the whole model at once. Because dendrites communicate with other dendrites via synaptic connections, the more connections you have in your brain, the better you can create mental models.

Help your learners absorb and understand complex concepts by leading up to them gradually. Think of Hansel and Gretel traveling through the forest—leave a trail of "idea crumbs" along the path of learning for students to follow. Start plotting the course before you even broach a new topic and continue directing learners about how to any apply and comprehend new ideas even after the subject's conclusion. Tap into any prior knowledge students will need to understand a topic days before you begin the lessons on it.

Suggestions

✔ Use graphic organizers, brainstorming sessions or group discussions to encourage everyone to contribute.
✔ Introduce vocabulary words and key ideas by posting them on the wall and using them in other lessons.
✔ Conduct discussions on related themes.
✔ Play word association games to trigger old thoughts and inspire new ones.
✔ Provide concrete examples and experiences of the new concept as early and as often as possible.

Which ideas did I try today? What were the results? What will I do differently next time?

_____

_____

_____

Active Breaks

Have on hand quick activities that pull students out of their chairs, increase their alertness and blood circulation and add some fun to the day. These short brain breaks (five minutes or less) help them consolidate new learning so they can remember it better later.

Suggestions

✔ **Getting to Know You Charades:** In pairs, learners communicate three personal facts to their partner without using words—only Charades gestures and movements are allowed. Or, participants could communicate three things about their school or their company, their personal job description or an idea for an activity during the training session.

✔ **Instant Replay:** This game heightens visual and auditory acuity by requiring participants to pay attention to details. In pairs, learners take turns acting out an idea (for five seconds) and mimicking (from memory) their partner's gestures. Add subject matter content to make it academically valuable. To add challenge for savvy learners, have students act out ideas for ten seconds or eliminate words from the acting and use gestures only.

✔ **City Night Sounds:** Put your audience into small teams. One team selects a set of sounds that might be heard at night in any big city. They perform their sounds for the whole group. One by one, send other teams to join them, adding other sounds and other people until you have the entire group enjoying a veritable nocturnal urban experience. Experiment with other auditory environments: have groups recreate the sounds of a junior high school, a jungle or an airport. Finish each reenactment with hearty applause.

Which ideas did I try today? What were the results? What will I do differently next time

_____

_____

_____

Eat Better to Improve Learning

Personal eating habits affect learning a great deal. Foods are a source of carbohydrates and sugar for energy, as well as the source of the proteins our bodies need to make amino acids. Foods provide the ingredients that either release or block the neurotransmitters that make us alert or drowsy—they even help us remember things! The time of day you schedule your meals and the order in which you eat certain foods has as much of an impact on your brain as the particular foods you select. The effects of diet on learning vary from person to person (influencing brain activity from as little as ten to as much as sixty-five percent), but the recommendations below will enhance to some degree the learning experience of anyone.

Suggestions

✔ Consume protein with carbohydrates to reduce the roller coaster cycle of sugar (energy) and insulin (lethargy) in the bloodstream.

✔ Eggs, wheat germ, salmon, unsaturated fats, brazil nuts, dark green leafy vegetables, apples, bananas and lean meats have all been shown to benefit brain function.

✔ Drink plenty of water between meals and a glass of water with meals.

✔ Eat smaller meals more frequently to provide a consistent supply of nutrients and energy to the brain throughout the day.

✔ Share nutritional information and discuss diet choices with adolescent and adult learners, and with parents at open house functions.

✔ Discuss good nutrition with younger learners and role model healthy snacks and habits in your own classroom.

**Which ideas did I try today? What were the results?
What will I do differently next time**

_____

_____

_____

Better Learning with Unguided Discussions

Is it better to conduct presenter-directed discussions or open, unguided, student-generated discussions? That depends on the topic. Younger students (up to the age of ten) learn better when you direct the course of an academic discussion. Older students (adolescents and adults) benefit from the opportunity to lead the discussions as a group. Studies suggest that the best way to motivate learners to change and develop their knowledge is to allow them time to conduct an unguided discussion on a topic—think Socratic seminar with a few ground rules. A discussion like this frees learners from feeling like they are being controlled or manipulated into believing what a teacher wants them to believe, and leaves them open to new ideas and behaviors.

Suggestions

✔ Have learners generate discussion questions for each topic. Give them the chance to generate test questions, too.

✔ At the outset of every new lesson, survey learners about what they'd actually like to learn from it. Incorporate as many of these interests into the content as you can.

✔ Activate prior knowledge to discover what learners already know about a topic. Observe student discussions or lead a group brainstorming session. With this information, you can avoid wasting class time on unnecessary review and use learners' backgrounds to enhance your lectures and activities.

✔ Allocate five to twenty percent of class time to small group discussions in partners or teams. Have learners debrief as a whole group or silently reflect in their journals at the end of each discussion.

Which ideas did I try today? What were the results? What will I do differently next time

_____

_____

_____

Enriched Environments Support Learning

Just how flexible is the human brain? Is it cemented for life or malleable enough to change? Astonishing research reveals that the brain not only can be modified by enriching experiences but also that change can occur in as few as four days! The brain responds to stimuli physically by growing new, larger, more extensive dendritic branches. It also releases growth factors, forms glial cells, boosts key neurotransmitters and supports both neurogenesis and better learning. Furthermore, this growth can happen in brains of any age, so long as they are properly stimulated.

Suggestions

✔ Introduce novelty and challenge to your classroom. Invite guest speakers, teach in new locales and incorporate props.

✔ Challenge and physical activity are among the most effective elements of an enriched environment. Ensure that students have enough time for walks, recess, games and P. E. on a daily basis. When you do play games, keep them challenging so that students don't become bored and the activity does not become a chore.

✔ Increase the feedback you provide to your learners. If you personally cannot give each student feedback at least once every thirty minutes, structure your course so that they get it from self-evaluations or peer interaction.

✔ Coordinate frequent positive social interaction. Let students work in pairs or small groups on some assignments.

✔ Design a stimulating physical environment with colorful, thought-provoking intervals, lots of hands-on activities and displays, aromas, music, multi-sensory experiences and flexible seating arrangements.

**Which ideas did I try today? What were the results?
What will I do differently next time**

_____

_____

_____

S-A-T: Not Just Another Exam!

The seven styles of communication range from one extreme to the other, some more effective than the rest—you can demand, threaten, tell, suggest, ask, imply or hope. Rarely will implying or hoping get your point across and it is usually inappropriate to demand or threaten. That leaves you with the options of suggesting, asking or telling—the S-A-T method. The tonalities, volume and tempo of the S-A-T method are direct without being menacing, which facilitates the best learning.

Suggestions

✔ Suggest to your audience that they are perfectly capable of performing a task, will learn it very easily and will find the learning personally valuable.

✔ Suggest that learners further explore a topic on their own time in greater detail, so they have the freedom to follow the path that most interests them.

✔ Ask learners to do things that they would want to do anyway to give them a sense of control and choice within the learning environment.

✔ Tell your learners to do things when you are short on time, but always explain why the outcome of the task is important to you and applies to them.

Which ideas did I try today? What were the results?
What will I do differently next time

_____

_____

_____

Brain Activators for the Visual Cortex

What activities will visually enrich the brain? Although many of the suggestions listed in this book are useful, the following few will specifically target the visual cortex.

Suggestions

✔ **Change environments**: Change student seats, move all the chairs to a different spot in the room, take a field trip, stand everyone up for one part of a lesson, hang new posters on the walls (or rearrange the ones that are already there) or decorate for the holidays.

✔ **Open the windows**: Research suggests that the brain benefits from views to natural environments and exterior scenery. You worry that students will be distracted if they can see outside? Maybe those who do look need an attention break or to be better engaged in the lesson.

✔ **Show and mimic games**: Play childhood games that require participants to copy gestures. Simon Says is one such game; there are many others.

✔ **Natural and incandescent lighting**: Are you sure that all you have available is fluorescent lighting? Can you change the bulbs or bring in other lamps? How about opening the curtains to flood the room with daylight? Or bringing your students outdoors or into better-lit rooms?

✔ **What's missing from this picture?** Alter one aspect of your room and challenge the whole group to identify the change. Put them into pairs to solve similar puzzles. Alternately, have a contest to see who can identify the most objects in the room.

Which ideas did I try today? What were the results?
What will I *do* differently next time

_____

_____

_____

Give Learners Environmental Options

Assigned seats may have some advantage for you but, in most cases, students perform better if they are given the choice to make their own selections. Research has found that up to twenty percent of all learners require mobility for optimal participation. These kinesthetic (tactile) learners often need to stand, move around or sit on the floor. Visual learners like to sit near the front of the room, or wherever the most visual information is displayed. Auditory learners enjoy working in cooperative groups; some auditory learners prefer to sit away from other people so they can concentrate. Even the side of the room you sit in affects what you take away from a lesson; learners sitting to the presenter's left will hear better out of their left ear, which will activate the right hemisphere of their brains; learners sitting to the presenter's right will end up activating the left hemisphere of their brains.

Suggestions

✔ Regularly change the side of the room from which you speak.
✔ Let learners sit in groups at least once a day.
✔ Alternate between individual and collaborative assignments.
✔ Give students the freedom to choose their seating for at least part of a lesson.
✔ Rearrange the entire chair, desk and table set-up to vary the classroom environment.

Which ideas did I try today? What were the results?
What will I do differently next time

_____

_____

_____

How to Grab the Brain's Attention

Two attention-getting biological mechanisms are built into the human brain, both for survival reasons. The first identifies change and novelty; large or sudden changes get the most attention. Trends (slow, gradual changes) are very poorly detected.

The second mechanism pays attention to emotionally dense information. Humans are riveted to scenes of tragedy, terror, exhilaration, suspense and sentiment. Perhaps you've noticed how the newspapers, television and entertainment media play up events like plane crashes, wars, homecomings, fierce competitions, high-speed auto chases and rescue missions. Smart presenters capitalize on these compelling, instinctive interests.

Suggestions

✔ Ask suspenseful questions, provide moving, personal examples of concepts and drop hints and teasers of ideas yet to be explained. For example, if you moved over the weekend, explain in science class how different it felt driving the tall, heavy moving van than your usual car.

✔ Have students give presentations—a change of faces at the front of the room is always a welcome event.

✔ Incorporate props, costumes and vocal changes. Have students wear costumes and use props, too.

✔ Dramatize and role-play course content to emphasize certain ideas.

✔ Add cliffhangers to lessons to grab and hold student interest. Read a particularly exciting or dramatic sentence from the next lesson ("Doctors believe that the only way to really avoid getting sick is to…"), stop at a suspenseful point and then put the text away.

Which ideas did I try today? What were the results? What will I do differently next time

_____

_____

_____

Laugh and Learn

Is laughing good for learning? Laughter increases the flow of neurotransmitters that are required for alertness and memory, lowers stress and strengthens the immune system. Laughter also provides a break in the routine and relaxes students who may be stressed or anxious. But should you turn your classroom into a comedy club? Use laughter as a part of a productive, energizing break rather than the major part of your presentation.

Suggestions

✔ Allow learner-added humor as long as it is in good taste and does not take away from content instruction time.

✔ Tell funny anecdotes or jokes to emphasize elements of a lesson.

✔ Keep a stash of funny videos, DVDs or audio clips on hand to play during tense or sluggish moments.

✔ Establish a ritual for daily or weekly joke-telling; students can address the whole class or exchange jokes in small groups.

✔ Display cartoons and comic strips on the wall or on the overhead, or include them on course handouts.

Which ideas did I try today? What were the results?
What will I *do* differently next time

_____

_____

_____

Use the Mind-Body Library of Knowledge

Our brain's library of knowledge is context dependent. Things we learn in one place are most easily accessed when we are in that same place. For example, have you ever been in the kitchen and remembered that you needed to get a book out of another room? You head down the hall for it and then suddenly realize you've forgotten what item you were going to get! Annoyed, you probably returned to the kitchen, physically retracing your steps until you stood in the same spot where you first thought of the book—and then remembered it was a book you wanted.

The same phenomenon works for mental contexts, too. Students who study for tests while relaxed won't do very well on the test if they are wound up when they take it. Students who study under high pressure and intensity will perform better on similarly stressful tests. The best thing you can do when you are assessing your students is plan ahead and put them into the same mental state before you hand them a test as you put them in when you taught and reviewed the material.

Suggestions

✔ Have students review their knowledge under the same conditions in which they would be tested on it. For example, give them a practice test with a timed deadline (they can work on it alone or with other students). When they take the real test, they'll be better prepared for the extra element of stress.

✔ Vary the stress levels of your class. Teach under low and moderate stress conditions to engage different types of test-takers.

✔ Before test time, de-stress students by having them stand to stretch, drink some water or doodle to clear their minds.

✔ Use a variety of testing and assessment methods to help students demonstrate what they have learned. You may vary the amount of time they have, the amount of privacy they have, the types of tools they can use (calculators or open book tests) or give them some choice about how they would like to be tested (written vs. oral assessment, participating in a formal discussion, demonstrating knowledge by solving a problem, et cetera).

✔ Make written tests more fun with cartoons, positive affirmations and test taking strategies in the white space on the pages. Perhaps question #12 would instruct test takers to take a deep breath, hold it for three counts and exhale, or to remind them to double-check their work.

Student Seating Matters

Student success hinges more on seating arrangements and chairs than you'd think! First, seating placement influences stress levels—students care very much about where they sit in the room and who they sit next to—and stress influences cognition. Second, classroom resources, like shared materials, lighting, hearing the teacher, warm or cool spots and noisy or quiet spots, can also be a source of stress. Finally, the shape of the chair or the tilt of the desk affects how comfortable it is to sit there. Students who are distracted or constantly shifting around to find a better posture or stretch a tired neck are not paying strict attention to academic concerns.

Suggestions

✔ Separate chairs and desks provide the best comfort and flexibility.
✔ Every ten or fifteen minutes, give students the chance to stretch muscles with a physical movement, anything from a stretching or cross-lateral exercise to walking across the room to meet in a group for a cooperative learning activity.
✔ Allow students to position themselves however they feel comfortable. Does it matter if a student lies on the floor or leans against the wall to read or takes a turn around the room with a partner as they discuss a question?
✔ Periodically, have students stand for two or three minutes while you teach, perhaps during a quick review or partner activity.
✔ Keep a variety of objects in the room to sit on, like an inflated exercise ball. Students who have sensory disorders, attention deficit or who are highly kinesthetic learners may sit better on the ball than a chair.

Which ideas did I try today? What were the results?
What will I do differently next time

_____

_____

_____

Too Hot to Learn?

The human brain is extremely sensitive to temperature. Research demonstrates that heat dramatically lowers scores on physical and intellectual tasks. Other studies show that reading comprehension declines when the temperature rises above 74 degrees Fahrenheit and math skills decline when it rises above 77 degrees! Extremely warm temperatures can increase lethargy in some people and anxiety or aggressiveness in others. To a point, when your brain is cooler, you feel more relaxed, receptive to new ideas and cognitively sharp. Classrooms kept between 68 and 72 degrees Fahrenheit are comfortable for the majority of students. In general, it is easier to adapt to a room that is too cold than one that is too hot. A temperature of 70 degrees Fahrenheit is ideal for learning situations that require focus and concentration, like reading and mathematics.

Suggestions

✔ If you don't have control of the temperature in your classroom, keep windows and doors open, direct fans across trays of water to cool the room, allow students to move around to find shady spots and urge students to dress in layers and stay hydrated.

✔ Attach a ribbon to an air vent or the window frame so you can tell at a glance if air is circulating.

✔ Decorating with blue and green colors will heighten a sense of cool.

**Which ideas did I try today? What were the results?
What will I do differently next time**

_____

_____

_____

Brighter Learning Prospects

Over the past century, the amount of outdoor light we are exposed to has generally declined. Ultraviolet light, present in sunshine, activates the synthesis of vitamin D, which aids in the absorption of essential minerals such as calcium; insufficient mineral intake has been shown to be a contributing factor in nonverbal cognitive deficiency. A large study of 21,000 schoolchildren from three districts in three states found that students with the most sunlight in their classrooms progressed 20 percent faster on math tests and 26 percent faster on reading tests compared to students exposed to the least amount of light.

Suggestions

✔ Limit students' extended exposure to darkened lecture halls and similar environments.

✔ During periods of limited sunlight (like during autumn and winter), take students on frequent brisk walks and have P. E. classes outdoors when weather permits (rather than in the gym).

✔ Open classroom blinds, doors and skylights.

✔ Take students outside for the occasional learning session. Not only will this expose them to more sunlight and fresh air, the novelty of learning in a new and different environment will stimulate their brains.

✔ Avoid direct sunlight or glare.

Which ideas did I try today? What were the results? What will I do differently next time

_____

_____

_____

Acoustics and Learning

The brain processes up to twenty thousand bits of auditory stimuli every second! Getting students to hear what we want them to hear in the classroom, therefore, can be a problem. In poorly designed classrooms that fail to address and reduce ambient noise—echo effects, reverberation and other acoustical problems—student attention, off-task behaviors and discipline problems increase. Sadly, many classrooms are acoustically unsound.

This issue takes a serious toll on learning. Classrooms can have enough background noise and echoes to hamper the learning of children with even mild hearing problems. Children in noisier areas have higher blood pressure, heart rates and elevated stress levels—none of which are conducive to learning. Reducing ambient noise helps students listen better and learn more

Suggestions

✔ Hang acoustic foam or tapestries on classroom walls to absorb noise and soften acoustics.

✔ Use soothing white noise or instrumental music to mask uncontrollable sound from air conditioning units or outdoors. White noise includes recordings of rainstorms, the bubble of a fish tank or the trickle of a desktop water fountain.

✔ Invest in a personal sound system to amplify your voice so every student can hear you.

✔ Mental concentration requires an especially quiet environment. Schedule tests and other intensive tasks during times when environmental noise levels are lowest.

✔ Move around the room so everyone gets the chance to hear you.

Which ideas did I try today? What were the results?
What will I do differently next time

_____

_____

_____

Time to Settle In

In-depth learning takes time to organize, integrate and store in the brain. Even visual images require time to process. The brain is limited in its ability to cycle through information; the process of learning occurs across multiple stages and it must occur in sequence. If learning stops at one particular stage, the process will not continue. New information must settle into the brain by passing through all the stages (through the frontal lobes, across the synapse, through the neurons and into the hippocampus) before any more can come in.

Settling time requires only one thing: freedom from new learning! Writing in journals or participating in a discussion is wonderful for helping the brain make meaning out of new information, but it is not settling time. The brain must rest. How much settling time it requires depends on the complexity of the information and how new the ideas are to the learner. The more familiar students are with the material and the easier it is to understand, the less settling time they need.

Suggestions

✔ If you teach very young children, schedule nap time or resting time to coincide with settling time.

✔ If you teach elementary school, assign classroom chores, send students to recess or lunch, give them five minutes to listen to quiet, instrumental music, assign an individual activity of their choice or let them walk in pairs around the room to give them time for information to cement itself.

✔ Complex, new material may require from two to five minutes of settling time every ten to fifteen minutes.

✔ Review content or simple material probably requires only one to two minutes of settling time every twenty to twenty-five minutes.

Which ideas did I try today? What were the results?
What will I do differently next time

_____

_____

_____

Setting Goals Improves Performance

Setting goals is one way to help learners maintain their focus and keep their concentration levels high. Goal setting primarily accomplishes two things: It focuses student attention on the task at hand and it provides the pleasure of anticipating the achievement of the goal, thereby stimulating the production of endorphins (the feel-good chemicals in the brain). To maximize the results of a goal-setting activity, follow the guidelines below.

Suggestions

✔ Although you may establish some of the criteria for setting goals, allow learners to set their own specific goals. They will be more meaningful to them and learners will be better inspired to reach for them.

✔ By definition a goal is a positive outcome that is specific and attainable. Set the standards for goals high enough so that students value achieving them but not so high that students are discouraged to even try to reach them in the time allotted.

✔ Have students list all the possible benefits they will experience when they reach their goals. Ask them to consider how they will feel upon success, how completing a goal would affect other people's opinions of their abilities and what personal gain they would receive. Tell students to answer the WIIFM question—What's in it for me?—to flesh out how accomplishing the goal will be beneficial.

✔ Encourage students to redefine their own goals as they work on them. Priorities and interests change as people become further invested in the process of working towards goals. Goals that are not reassessed and revised are in danger of becoming meaningless.

✔ Do not offer rewards to students who reach the goals they have set for themselves. Instead, work with students to make their goals meaningful and valuable, so they discover intrinsic motivation to pursue them.

Which ideas did I try today? What were the results?
What will I do differently next time

_____

_____

_____

Make Unforgettable Memories

"Contamination" is one of the biggest learning problems facing students and presenters. Ideas and topics become contaminated when too many of them are introduced in the same location—memories of where one fact begins and another ends all start running into each other. The brain needs distinct contexts for distinct concepts. If you sat in the same seat in the same lecture hall listening to the same professor and taking notes in the same notebook for an entire semester, don't you think that after a while it would be hard to keep it all straight in your memory?

Avoid contaminating learning by creating as many separate learning contexts as you can, either by altering a circumstance or location. Almost nobody could say exactly where he was on July 19, 1969, but lots of people could tell you where they were on July 20, 1969—the day of the first landing on the moon. We easily recall the events that occur on birthdays, anniversaries and vacations, too. The more distinctive you can make the environment of your classroom on different days or for different units, the more likely it is that your learners will remember things they learn.

Suggestions

✔ Give students the freedom to change seats (their location within the room) to help them vary their learning context.

✔ Change where you stand in the room to deliver instruction. Switch with every new unit or at important moments in a lesson.

✔ Allow learners to choose their seats during tests (as long as you ensure that each learner will have sufficient privacy no matter where she sits).

✔ Utilize props, costumes and accessories during presentations and group activities to add contextual details to learning memories.

✔ Engage emotions to distinguish learned ideas and concepts from each other. Stage debates and arguments, write in journals, plan role-playing assignments and give time for students to tell personal stories about ways learning has become relevant to their lives.

Encourage Faster Learning with Pre-Exposure

The brain readily absorbs small parcels of new information, one relevant iota at a time. It has trouble, though, immediately comprehending new ideas, new subjects or paradigm shifts. Anything we know well we learned over time, never all at once (downloading skills directly into the brain is still the stuff of science fiction!). Still, educators have very little time to present information in easily digestible pieces. Pre-exposing students to material is one strategy that gives them glimpses of new concepts and brief experiences of upcoming content far in advance of the moment they will need to actively gather information about these topics.

Television programs and movie theaters are rife with trailers of upcoming shows and series. Commercials and previews entice viewers with outrageous sound bites or hint at unresolved plots to encourage them to tune into the next episode or buy a ticket to a film. Tease your learners' interest in new material the same way. Once they are hooked by a puzzle, mystery or fascinating fact, they have some mental structure—think of it as Velcro® in the brain—to which they can attach meaning and comprehension of the topic when you present it in the future.

Suggestions

✔ Display a mural or graphic organizer about upcoming content two to four weeks in advance of its scheduled appearance in your curriculum.

✔ Continually provide examples of subjects, topics and ideas that you'll discuss in the near future.

✔ Schedule a guest speaker or show a video on a topic well in advance of your first lesson.

✔ Have learners research some topic that will provide the background information they need to understand another topic.

✔ Conduct brainstorming sessions or small group activities that enable students to gather everything they already know about an upcoming topic, as well as draft questions about what they would like to learn during the unit.

Do Learners Know What They Know?

We learn without trying to, sometimes without even being aware of it. It's altogether different to be consciously aware about the extent of our knowledge—that is, to know that we know it. Many people have no idea how they gained the knowledge they have or what to do to increase it.

Instructors can help such learners by providing them with three things: 1) review or reinforcement in their preferred learning modality (auditory, visual or kinesthetic); 2) multiple ways to practice and demonstrate learning, so they can review it several times in several formats; and 3) review time that is extended enough for learners to really internalize information, rather than stash it in their short-term memory until the end of a class or after they've regurgitated it to a test. You'll know when a learner has finally knowingly grasped a concept or solved a problem; satisfaction radiates from their expression and posture as they enjoy the "Aha!" moment of discovery.

Suggestions

✔ Provide review in multiple learning modalities. Make sure everyone sees, hears and physically acts out or touches the reinforcement. One day, you might have small groups work on graphic organizers; another day, you could give them clay so they could create a model of a concept; a third day you could play a question-answer game or conduct a discussion.

✔ Ensure that learners have the opportunity to experience new learning several different times. Perhaps follow a peer teaching assignment immediately with another one, this time with different partners.

✔ Add celebration to the learning process. Allow learners who have achieved significant milestones select the background music for a particular activity, receive special congratulations or take a moment to enjoy pride in their accomplishments.

**Which ideas did I try today? What were the results?
What will I do differently next time?**

_____

_____

_____

Smart Activators for the Auditory Cortex

Studies of musicians and brain-based phonological training programs show that when areas of the auditory cortex are continually stimulated in a meaningful way, the brain actually increases mass in that area. This suggests significant plasticity in the brain (or the ability to change its neural map). The key factor behind these changes seems to be coherence and repetition. Whether children are learning to read and speak or are developing balance, posture and coordination, this area of the brain is crucial to development. Research suggests that combining sounds and activities in many ways is good for the brain. Perform auditory activities often and provide plenty of explanation so that learners understand the reasoning behind them.

Suggestions

✔ **Repetition:** Repetition is good for the brain, but "drill and thrill" students rather than "drill and kill." Make repetitions interesting, relevant and challenging. Repeat key ideas with a twist, repeat songs in a new way, repeat rhymes, repeat rituals and repeat good habits.

✔ **Singing songs:** The easiest time to convince learners to sing songs is before second grade or during choir class. Older learners can sing school songs or rewrite the lyrics to a pop song and sing it as to review content.

✔ **Active listening:** Preview songs to teach vocabulary. Play one three times in a row and ask students to listen for new words each time you play it. Or, play songs as a listening exercise; ask participants to listen carefully to an entire song and then write out its chorus. This improves concentration and working memory.

✔ **Playing and making music:** Bring instruments to class and allow students to bring their own. Express ideas through music a few minutes each day. Play music from all eras and places so students can learn how music was composed during other times in history or across the world.

✔ **Sensory awareness:** Ask students to move slowly across the room and identify all the sensations they experience (sight, sound, taste, touch and smell). Or, have them close their eyes and identify all the sounds they hear while sitting still for three minutes. To conclude, ask students to list everything they experienced and compare their lists to a partner's.

Appendix

Bibliography

Allen, C. K. (1990, Aug). Encoding of colors in short-term memory. *Perceptual and Motor Skills,* 71(1), 211–5.

Amabile, T. & Rovee-Collier, C. (1991, Oct). Contextual variation and memory retrieval at six months. *Child Development,* 62(5), 1155–66.

Ames, C. (1992). Classrooms: Goals, structures, and student motivation. *Journal of Educational Psychology,* 84, 261–71.

Asbjornsen, A., Hugdahl, K., & Hynd, G. W. (1990, Oct). The effects of head and eye turns on the right ear advantage in dichotic listening. *Brain and Language,* 39(3), 447–58.

Backman, L., Nilsson, L. G., & Nourp, R. K. (1993, Sept). Attentional demands and recall of verbal and color information in action events. *Scandinavian Journal of Psychology,* 34(3), 246–54.

Bahrick, H. P. & Hall, L. K (1991). Lifetime maintenance of high school mathematics content. *Journal of Experimental Psychology: General,* 120, 20–33.

Black J. E., Isaacs, K. R., Anderson, B. J., Alcantara, A. A., & Greenough, W. T. (1990, July). Learning causes synaptogenesis, whereas motor activity causes angiogenesis, in cerebral cortex of adult rats. *Proceedings of the National Academy of Sciences* (USA), 87, 5568–72.

Boller, K. & Rovee-Collier, C. (1992, Feb). Contextual coding and recoding of infant's memories. *Journal of Experimental Child Psychology,* 53(1), 1–23.

Botella, J. & Eriksen, C. W. (1992, Apr). Filtering versus parallel processing in RSVP tasks. *Perception and Psychophysics,* 51(4), 334–43.

Bower, G. H. & Mann, T. (1992, Nov). Improving recall by recoding interfering material at the time of retrieval. *Journal of Experimental Psychology,* 18(6), 1310–20.

Bower, G. H. & Morrow, G. (1990, Jan 5). Mental models in narrative comprehension. *Science,* 247(4938), 44–8.

Braun, C. M. (1992, Dec). Estimation of interhemispheric dynamics from simple unimanual reaction time to extrafoveal stimuli. *Neuropsychology Review,* 3(4), 321–65.

Caine, R. N. & Caine, G. (1994). *Making Connections: Teaching and the Human Brain.* Menlo Park, CA: Addison-Wesley.

Capaldi, E. J. & Neath, I. (1995). Remembering and forgetting as context discrimination. *Learning and Memory,* 2(3–4), 107–32.

Carpenter, G. A. & Grossberg, S. (1993, Apr). Normal and amnesic learning, recognition and memory by a model of corticohippocampal interactions. *Trends in Neurosciences,* 16(4), 131–7.

Carper, Jean (1993). *Food: Your Miracle Medicine.* New York, NY: HarperCollins Publishers.

Christianson, S. A. (1992, Sept). Emotional stress and eyewitness memory: A critical review. *Psychological Bulletin,* 112(2), 284–309.

Chugani, H. T. & Phelps, M. E. (1991, Jan). Imaging human brain development with positron emission tomography. *Journal of Nuclear Medicine,* 32(1), 23–6.

Coward, L. Andrew (1990). *Pattern Thinking.* New York, NY: Praeger Publishers.

Csikszentmihalyi, M. (1990). *Flow: The Psychology of Optimal Experience.* New York, NY: Harper & Row.

Damasio, Antonio (1994). *Descartes' Error: Emotion, Reason, and the Human Brain.* New York, NY: Putnam & Sons.

Davidson, R. J. (1992, Sept). Anterior cerebral asymmetry and the nature of emotion. *Brain and Cognition,* 20(1), 125–51.

Decety, J. & Ingvar, D. H. (1990, Feb). Brain structures participating in mental simulation of motor behavior: A neuropsychological interpretation. *Acta Psychologica,* 73(1),13–34.

Dennison, Paul & Dennison, Gail (1994). *Brain Gym (Teacher's Edition Revised).* Ventura, CA: Edu-Kinesthetics.

Dossey, Larry (1993). *Healing Words: The Power of Prayer and the Practice of Medicine.* San Francisco, CA: HarperCollins.

Dunn, R., Dunn, K., & Treffinger, D. (1992). *Bringing Out the Giftedness in Your Child: Nurturing Every Child's Unique Strengths, Talents, and Potential.* New York, NY: John Wiley & Sons.

Eich, E. (1995). Searching for mood dependent memory. *Psychological Science,* 6, 67–75.

Engel, A. K., Konig, P., Kreiter, A. K., Schillen, T. B., & Singer, W. (1992, Jun). Temporal coding in the visual cortex: New vistas on integration in the nervous system. *Trends in Neurosciences*, 15(6), 218–26.

Eysenck, Michael (Ed.) (1994). *The Blackwell Dictionary of Cognitive Psychology*. Oxford, UK: Blackwell.

Fabiani M., Karis, D., & Donchin, E. (1990, Feb). Effects of mnemonic strategy manipulation in a Von Restorff paradigm. *Electroencephalography and Clinical Neurophysiology*, 75(2), 22–35.

Fitch, R. H., Brown, C. P., & Tallal, P. (1993, Jun 14). Left hemisphere specialization for auditory temporal processing in rats. *Annals of the New York Academy of Sciences*, 682, 346–7.

Fox, N. A. (1991, Aug). If it's not left, it's right. Electroencephalograph asymmetry and the development of emotion. *The American Psychologist*, 46(8), 863–72.

Fuchs, J. L., Montemayor, M., & Greenough, W. T. (1990, Sept). Effect of environmental complexity on size of the superior colliculus. *Behavioral and Neural Biology*, 54(2), 198–203.

Goleman, Daniel (1995). *Emotional Intelligence: Why It Can Matter More than IQ*. New York, NY: Bantam Books.

Gratton, G., Coles, M. G., & Donchin, E. (1992, Dec). Optimizing the use of information: strategic control of activation of responses. *Journal of Experimental Psychology: General*, 121(4), 480–506.

Greenough, W. T. & Anderson, B. J. (1991). Cerebellar synaptic plasticity. Relation to learning versus neural activity. *Annals of the New York Academy of Sciences*, 627, 231–47.

Greenough, W. T., Withers, G., & Anderson, B. (1992). Experience-dependent synaptogenesis as a plausible memory mechanism. In I. Gormezano & E. Wasserman (Eds.), *Learning and Memory: The Behavioral and Biological Substrates* (pp. 209–29). Hillsdale, NJ: Erlbaum & Associates.

Grunwald, L. & Goldberg, J. (1993, July). Babies are smarter than you think. *Life*, 45–60.

Hannaford, Carla (1995). *Smart Moves: Why Learning Is Not All in Your Head*. Arlington, VA: Great Ocean Publishers.

Harth, Erich (1995). *The Creative Loop: How the Brain Makes a Mind*. Reading, MA: Addison-Wesley.

Hassler, M. (1991). Testosterone and musical talent. *Experimental and Clinical Endocrinology*, 98(2), 89–98.

Healy, Alice & Bourne, Lyle (1995). *Learning and Memory of Knowledge and Skills: Durability and Specificity*. Thousand Oaks, CA: Sage Publications.

Healy, J. M. (1990). *Endangered Minds: Why Our Children Don't Think*. New York, NY: Simon and Schuster.

Healy, J. M. (1994). *Your Child's Growing Mind: A Guide to Learning and Brain Development from Birth to Adolescence*. New York, NY: Doubleday.

Hirsch, A. (1993). *Floral Odor Increases Learning Ability*. Paper presented at the annual conference of American Academy of Neurological & Orthopedic Surgery.

Hobson, J. A. (1994). *The Chemistry of Conscious States: How the Brain Changes Its Mind*. New York, NY: Little, Brown & Company.

Horn, G. (1991, Jan). Learning, memory and the brain. *Indian Journal of Physiology and Pharmacology*, 35(1), 3–9.

Horne, J. (1992, Oct 15). Human slow wave sleep: A review and appraisal of recent findings, with implications for sleep functions, and psychiatric illness. *Experientia*, 48(10), 941–54.

Howard, Pierce (1994). *The Owner's Manual for the Brain*. Austin, TX: Leornian Press.

Huttenlocher, P. R. (1990). Morphometric study of human cerebral cortex development. *Neuropsychologia*, 28(6), 517–27.

Iaccino, James (1993). *Left Brain—Right Brain Differences: Inquiries, Evidence, and New Approaches*. Hillsdale, NJ: Lawrence Erlbaum & Associates.

Introini-Collision, I. B., Miyazaki, B., & McGaugh, J. L. (1991). Involvement of the amygdala in the memory-enhancing effects of clenbuterol. *Psychopharmacology* (Berlin), 104(4), 541–4.

Isaacs, K. R., Anderson, B. J., Alcantara, A. A., Black, J. E., & Greenough, W. T. (1992, Jan). Exercise and the brain: Angiogenesis in the adult rat cerebellum after vigorous physical activity and motor skill learning. *Journal of Cerebral Blood Flow and Metabolism*, 12(1), 110–9.

Jacobs, B., Schall, M., & Scheibel, A. B. (1993). A quantitative dendritic analysis of Wernicke's area in humans. II. Gender, hemispheric, and environmental factors. *Journal of Comparative Neurology*, 327(1), 97–111.

Jensen, Eric (1994). *The Learning Brain*. Thousand Oaks, CA: Corwin Press.

Jensen, Eric (1995). *Brain-Based Learning and Teaching*. Thousand Oaks, CA: Corwin Press.

Jernigan, T. L. & Tallal, P. (1990, May). Late childhood changes in brain morphology observable with MRI. *Developmental Medicine and Child Neurology*, 32(5), 379–85.

Kandel, M. & Kandel, E. (1994, May). Flights of memory. *Discover*, 32–8.

Kandel, E. & Hawkins, R. (1992, Sept). The biological basis of learning and individuality. *Scientific American,* 267(3), 79–86.

Kenyon, Tom (1994). *Brain States.* Naples, FL: United States Publishing.

Klutky, N. (1990). [Sex differences in memory performance for odors, tone sequences and colors.] *Zeitscrift fur Experimentelle und Angewandte Psychologie* (German), 37(3), 437–46.

Kohn, A. (1993). *Punished by Rewards: The Trouble with Gold Stars, Incentive Plans, A's, Praise, and Other Bribes.* Boston, MA: Houghton Mifflin.

Kosslyn, Steven & Koenig, Oliver (1992). *Wet Mind: The New Cognitive Neuroscience.* New York, NY: Free Press.

Kotulak, Ronald (1993, April 11) Unraveling hidden mysteries of the brain. *Chicago Tribune,* p. 11.

Levine, S. C., Jordan, N. C., & Huttenlocher, J. (1992, Feb). Development of calculation abilities in young children. *Journal of Experimental Child Psychology,* 53(1), 72–103.

Lewicki, P., Hill, T., & Czyzewska, M. (1992, June). Nonconscious acquisition of information. *American Psychologist,* 47(6), 796–801.

Maguire, J. (1990). *Care and Feeding of the Brain: A Guide to Your Gray Matter.* New York, NY: Doubleday.

Martin, R. C. (1993, Mar). Short-term memory and sentence processing: Evidence from neuropsychology. *Memory and Cognition,* 21(2), 176–83.

McGaugh J. L., Introini-Collision, I. B., Nagahara, A. H., Cahill, L., Brioni, J. D., & Castellano, C. (1990). Involvement of the amygdaloid complex in neuromodulatory influences on memory storage. *Neuroscience and Biobehavioral Reviews,* 14(4), 425–31.

Meece, J. L., Wigfield, A., & Eccles, J. S. (1990). Predictors of math anxiety and its influence on young adolescents' course enrollment intentions and performance in mathematics. *Journal of Educational Psychology,* 82, 60–70.

Michaud, Ellen & Wild, Russell (1991). *Boost Your Brain Power: A Total Program to Sharpen Your Thinking and Age-Proof Your Mind.* Emmaus, PA: Rodale Press.

Nadel, L. (1990). Varieties of spatial cognition. Psychobiological considerations. *Annals of the New York Academy of Sciences,* 608, 613–26.

Nakamura, K. (1993). A theory of cerebral learning regulated by the reward system. I. Hypotheses and mathematical description. *Biological Cybernetics,* 68(6), 491–8.

Neisser, Ulric & Harsch, Nicole (1992). Phantom flashbulbs: False recollections of hearing the news about Challenger. In E. Winograd & U. Neisser (Eds.), *Affect and Accuracy in Recall: Studies of "Flashbulb" Memories* (pp. 9–31). New York, NY: Cambridge UP.

Olds, James (1992). Mapping the mind onto the brain. In F. Worden, J. Swazey, & G. Adelman (Eds.), *The Neurosciences, Paths of Discovery.* Boston, MA: Birkhauser.

Orlock, Carol (1993). *Inner Time: The Science of Body Clocks and What Makes Us Tick.* New York, NY: Carol Publishing Group.

Ostrander, Sheila & Schroeder, Lynn (1991). *Supermemory: The Revolution.* New York, NY: Carroll & Graf Publishers.

Pulvirenti, L. (1992). Neural plasticity and memory: Towards an integrated view. *Functional Neurology,* 7(6), 481–90.

Roland, P. E., Gulyas, B., Seitz, R. J., Bohm, C., & Stone-Elander, S. (1990, Sept). Functional anatomy of storage, recall and recognition of a visual pattern in man. *Neuroreport,* 1(1), 53–6.

Rose, F. D., Davey, M. J., & Attree, E. A. (1993, Feb). How does environmental enrichment aid performance following cortical injury in the rat? *Neuroreport,* 4(2), 163–6.

Rose, Steven (1993). *The Making of Memory: From Molecules to Mind.* New York, NY: Anchor.

Rosenfield, M. & Ciuffreda, K. J. (1991, Jan). Effect of surround propinquity on the open-loop accommodative response. *Investigative Ophthalmology and Visual Science,* 32(1), 142–7.

Rosenfield, M. & Gilmartin, B. (1990, Feb). Effect of target proximity on the open-loop accommodative response. *Optometry and Vision Science,* 67(2), 74–9.

Rossi, E. L. & Nimmons, D. (1991). *The 20-Minute Break: Reduce Stress, Maximize Performance, and Improve Health and Emotional Well-Being Using the New Science of Ultradian Rhythms.* Los Angeles, CA: Tarcher.

Schab, F. R. (1990, July). Odors and the remembrance of things past. *Journal of Experimental Psychology: Learning, Memory and Cognition,* 16(4), 648–655.

Schacter, D. L. (1992, Apr). Understanding implicit memory. A cognitive neuroscience approach. *American Psychologist*, 47(4), 559–69.

Schatz, C. J. (1992, Sept). The developing brain. *Scientific American: Special Issue on the Mind and Brain*, 267(3), 60–7.

Schatz, C. J. (1990). Impulse activity and the patterning of connections during CNS development. *Neuron*, 5(6), 745–56.

Schneider, W. (1993, Mar). Varieties of working memory as seen in biology and in connectionist/control architectures. *Memory and Cognition*, 21(2), 184–92.

Schunk, D. H. (1990). Goal setting and self-efficacy during self-regulated learning. *Educational Psychologist*, 25(1), 71–86.

Sirevaag, A. M. & Greenough, W. T. (1991). Plasticity of GFAP-immunoreactive astrocyte size and number in visual cortex of rats reared in complex environments. *Brain Research*, 540(1–2), 273–8.

Smith, A. P., Kendrick, A. M., & Maben, A. L. (1992). Effects of breakfast and caffeine on performance and mood in the late morning and after lunch. *Neuropsychobiology*, 26(4), 198–204.

Smith, B. D., Davidson, R. A., & Green, R. L. (1993, Sept). Effects of caffeine and gender on physiology and performance: Further tests of a biobehavioral model. *Physiology and Behavior*, 54(3), 415–22.

Squire, L. R. (1992, Apr). Memory and the hippocampus: A synthesis from findings with rats, monkeys, and humans. *Psychological Review*, 99(2), 195–231.

Squire, L. (1995, May 10). Mystery of memory. *San Diego Union*, E-1–4.

Sullivan, R. M., McGaugh, J. L. & Leon, M. (1991). Norepinephrine-induced plasticity and one-trial olfactory learning in neonatal rats. *Brain Research: Developmental Brain Research*, 60(2), 219–28.

Sylwester, R. (1995). *A Celebration of Neurons: An Educator's Guide to the Human Brain*. Alexandria, VA: ASCD.

Tallal, P. (1991). Hormonal influences in developmental learning disabilities. *Psychoneuroendocrinology*, 16(1–3), 203–11.

Tallal, P., Miller, S., & Fitch, R. H. (1993). Neurobiological basis of speech: A case for the preeminence of temporal processing. *Annals of the New York Academy of Sciences*, 682, 27–47.

Thal, D. J. & Tobias, S. (1992, Dec). Communicative gestures in children with delayed onset of oral expressive vocabulary. *Journal of Speech and Hearing Research*, 35(6), 1281–9.

Thal, D. J., Tobias, S., & Morrison, D. (1991, Jun). Language and gesture in late talkers: A 1-year follow-up. *Journal of Speech and Hearing Research*, 34(3), 604–12.

Thompson, Richard. (1993). *The Brain: A Neuroscience Primer*. New York, NY: W. H. Freeman.

Trevarthen, Colwyn (1990). Growth and education of the hemispheres. In C. Trevarthen, *Brain Circuits and Functions of the Mind: Essays in Honor of Roger W. Sperry* (pp. 334–63). New York, NY: Cambridge UP.

Uhl, F., Goldenberg, G., Lang, W., Lindinger, G., Steiner, M., & Deecke, L. (1990). Cerebral correlates of imagining colours, faces and a map—II. Negative cortical DC potentials. *Neuropsychologia*, 28(1), 81–93.

Urban, M. J. (1992, Apr). Auditory subliminal stimulation: A re-examination. *Perceptual and Motor Skills*, 74(2), 515–41.

Vincent, J. D. (1990). *The Biology of Emotions*. Cambridge, MA: Basil Blackwell.

Wallace, C. S., Kilman, V. L., Withers, G. S., & Greenough, W. T. (1992, July). Increases in dendritic length in occipital cortex after 4 days of differential housing in weanling rats. *Behavioral and Neural Biology*, 58(1), 64–8.

Webb, D. & Webb, T. (1990). *Accelerated Learning with Music*. Norcross, GA: Accelerated Learning Systems.

Wenger, Win (1992). *Beyond Teaching and Learning: Ways to Profoundly Improve the Experience and Results of Learning*. Gaithersburg, MD: Psychegenic Press.

Wenger, Win (1995). *The Einstein Factor: A Proven New Method for Increasing Your Intelligence*. Rocklin, CA: Prima.

Wurtman, R. J. (1990). Carbohydrate craving. Relationship between carbohydrate intake and disorders of mood. *Drugs*, 39(Suppl 3), 49–52.

Suggested Additional Readings From Corwin Press

10 Best Teaching Practice , 2nd Ed. (2005) by Donna Walker Tileston

12 Brain/Mind Learning Principles in Action (2005) by Renate Nummela Caine, Geoffrey Caine, Carol McClintic, and Karl Klimek

A Biological Brain in a Cultural Classroom, 2nd Ed. (2003) by Robert Sylvester

Becoming a "Wiz" at Brain-Based Teaching (2002) by Marilee Sprenger

Brain-Based Learning (2000) by Eric Jensen

Brain-Based Learning, The Video Program for How the Brain Learns, Featuring David A. Sousa (2000)

Building the Reading Brain, PreK-3 (2004) by Patricia Wolfe and Pamela Nevills

Classroom Activators: 64 Novel Ways to Energize Learners (2004) by Jerry Evanski

Designing Brain-Compatible Learning, 2nd Ed. (2003) by Terrence Parry and Gayle Gregory

Environments for Learning (2003) by Eric Jensen

How the Brain Learns, 3rd Ed. (2006) by David A. Sousa

How the Brain Learns to Read (2005) by David A. Sousa

How the Brain Learns/Como Aprende el Cerebro, 2nd Ed./Segunda Edicion (2002) by David A. Sousa

How the Gifted Brain Learns (2003) by David A. Sousa

How the Special Needs Brain Learns (2001) by David A. Sousa

How to Explain a Brain (2005) by Robert Sylvester

Introduction to Brain-Compatible Learning (1998) by Eric Jensen

Learning Smarter (2001) by Eric Jensen and Michael Dabney

Learning with the Body in Mind (2000) by Eric Jensen

Mindful Learning (2003) by Linda Campbell

Music With the Brain in Mind (2000) by Eric Jensen

Sensorcises: Active Enrichment for the Out-of-Step Learner (2004) by Laurie Glazener

Sizzle and Substance (1998) by Eric Jensen

The Leadership Brain (2003) by David A. Sousa

Tools for Engagement (2003) by Eric Jensen

Trainer's Bonanza (1998) by Eric Jensen

TrainSmart: Perfect Trainings Every Time (2001) by Rich Allen

About the Author

Eric Jensen has taught at the elementary, middle school and senior high school level, as well as at three California universities. In 1981, he co-founded SuperCamp, the country's most successful brain-compatible learning program for students. He helped introduce brain-based learning to Australia, Denmark, New Zealand, Sweden and South Africa. Jensen has authored twenty-two books, including the best-selling *Teaching with the Brain in Mind, Super Teaching, Tools for Engagement, The Learning Brain* and *Brain-Based Learning*. He speaks at many major conferences; his work has been featured in *USA Today*, the *Wall Street Journal* and on CNN. He is currently a staff developer and member of the Society for Neuroscience.

Notes:

Notes:

**CORWIN
PRESS**

The Corwin Press logo—a raven striding across an open book—represents the union of courage and learning. Corwin Press is committed to improving education for all learners by publishing books and other professional development resources for those serving the field of PreK–12 education. By providing practical, hands-on materials, Corwin Press continues to carry out the promise of its motto: **"Helping Educators Do Their Work Better."**